Creating PA NDAU Appliqué

A New Approach to an Ancient Art Form

Carla J. Hassel

Photographs: Hetherington Studio,
unless otherwise credited.

Cover Design and Layout: Heather Miller

Copyright ©1984
Carla J. Hassel

Library of Congress
Catalog Card Number 83-051586

ISBN 0-87069-390-5
10 9 8 7 6 5 4 3 2

Published by

Wallace-Homestead Book Company
580 Water's Edge Road
Lombard, Illinois 60148

This book is dedicated to Mai Chao Vang, Mao Thor Lee, May Yang, Se Vang, Sao Thao Lee, Chia Lor, and Chue Vang, who prove with every day of their lives that determination and hope will win in the end.

Many Thanks

This project became many projects before much time had passed, as every waking moment became entangled with some aspect of the Hmong's needs. So many people are now deserving of my gratitude and appreciation.

To Ann Jennings and Katy Hoover, for the hours spent with "the ladies," and more hours spent listening to me as I sorted out my thoughts.

To Janis Waldorf and Dorothy Judge, who shared their Ginghers and Berninas with the ladies in the Plymouth Church basement when we needed results, and fast.

To Alden Hebard, who said "yes" when I needed immediate solutions. He never asked the predictable "why's."

To Kirsten and David, who gave up a spring vacation to teach color words and theory, who packaged three hundred pa ndau kits when the swimming pool beckoned that 100-degree day, and who did so much more.

To Ken McDougal, who found a way to make the dream of pa ndau kits a marketable reality.

To Linda Jones, who found a grant for *Covenant*, the masterpiece the ladies will create.

To Carter Houck and Myron Miller, who dropped in one day during Crisis Number 299 and made the whole project seem worth the effort despite the setbacks. They *made* me write this book.

To Dick Pommrehn, who helped in the quietest of ways.

To Joy Kidney, who nursed along the beginnings of the book when we returned to dormitory life for a week during the hottest summer since 1936, and who was the first to wade through the rudiments of pa ndau terminology. She is a never-ending source of inspiration and support.

To the artists, Heather Miller and Jann Williams, who made everything look just right; to the photographers, Myron Miller, Mike Fletcher, and John and Doug Hetherington, who made everything appear so real; and to my fletch, Liz Fletcher, who kept the book project on course.

To June Pyle who, in four days or less, shared the joy of pa ndau with what must have been half the world. She chants, "No, it isn't a mola" in her sleep.

To Margaret Ireland, who capitalized, uncapitalized, and recapitalized snailhouse (no, Snailhouse!) as though she enjoyed it.

To Thai Lee, who counseled and researched and nit-picked with me on every detail and told me without flinching that I am an "old lady." A braver soul never ate rice!

Enormous measures of gratitude go to three very special people. Cynthia Rehm, truly a guardian angel, who appears when the going gets too rough for mere mortals and sets the machinery back in motion. Jim Leimkuhler, who perhaps knows me better than I like, but put up with me and my wild ideas despite the madness, believing that this book needed to be written. Gary, who answers the foreign language phone calls at 11:30 at night and at 6:00 in the morning with nary a grumble, who has learned to like a dozen different rices ranging from sticky to stinky, who listens patiently and then tells me what I really said, and who deserves far better than all the hassles.

The success of the Hmong project(s) is due largely to the combined efforts of many. Perhaps a happy ending is just around the corner.

Contents

Who Are the Hmong and What Is Pa nDau?

The Hmong (pronounced mung) are an ancient tribe of mountain people who migrated from China in the mid-nineteenth century in search of freedom and a land of their own. Indeed, the word Hmong means "free." The freedom they cherish is an all-encompassing liberty that means far more than independence from a political government or a system of economics. It is a freedom of the spirit, a freedom to be their own people, and it is the very essence of their being. When they left China, they settled in the upper mountain regions of what are now Laos, Thailand, and North Vietnam. Theirs was a primitive agrarian culture and the language was unwritten. The only contact with the progressing outside world was through the young men who traveled to the cities in the lowlands to market their goods and buy the supplies they could not produce on their own.

As in virtually all cultures, the women turned to folk art as a brightener in the tedium of day-to-day existence. Like their fellow folk artists, they found mental and physical therapy in needlework as they added design and color to useful household items. They also found peace, pride, and self-worth. Their needlework techniques were as primitive as their farming, yet they developed and perfected geometric cross-stitch designs, crewelwork, embroidery, and reverse appliqué. They called all of these forms of needlework *pa ndau* (pronounced pond-ouw), regardless of the technique or combination of techniques they used. Pa ndau actually means "flower cloth," but the term today refers to any textile decorated to be as beautiful as a garden of flowers.

Historically, the women had virtually no contact with women outside their own villages and tribe. In spite of this isolation, they shared a basic foundation of techniques and products. Minute, counted cross-stitches appear on belts for both men and women. Reverse appliqué and cross-stitch are used to decorate the *nyia* (pronounced knee-ah), a flat cover with bindings that is used to carry a newborn baby, papoose-style. As the children come of age, they are presented with ceremonial vests constructed on a black fabric base with horizontal strips of exquisite reverse appliqué, appliqué, embroidery, and, often, dangling tin "coins." The geometric reverse appliqué designs decorate garments, tablecloths, and walls. With time, individuals and families selected favorite designs and elaborated upon them. As they stitched and visited with one another, many of the women gave names to the patterns. To others, names were irrelevant. In several instances, the women attributed symbolic meaning to some of the basic designs, magnifying the already substantial sentimental significance of the art form. Naturally such symbolism varied from village to village and from clan to clan. In some regions, no symbolism was attached to the designs at all.

During the Vietnam war, many of the Hmong men aided the CIA and befriended American soldiers, risking their lives and marking themselves for the future retaliation that would ultimately drive them from their homelands in Laos, Cambodia, and Vietnam to refugee camps in Thailand. Many have immigrated to this country, bringing with them few belongings, but a wealth of heritage and the strong bonds of family and tribal unity. The women also brought pa ndau.

Of all the pa ndau forms, the one most noteworthy to the American quiltmaker is the geometric reverse appliqué. This technique does not involve quilting per se, because quilting in the strictest sense implies the stitching together of three layers: the top (simple, pieced, or appliquéd), a batting, and a backing. In pa ndau, an overlay is reverse-appliquéd to a background fabric, creating the design. This stitching simultaneously anchors the design to a foundation layer. Therefore, although there are three layers as in traditional quilting, the stitching is done only once.

Just as *molas*, pictorial reverse appliqué stitcheries of the San Blas Indians, have been appreciated and assimilated by American quiltmakers, the geometric reverse appliqué of the Hmong is gaining recognition as an important new art form. The designs and techniques are so fascinating that quiltmakers and other needle artists are eager to study the craft and attempt it on their own.

Symbolism and nomenclature

In spite of the regional preferences and localized communication of the Hmong, many pa ndau reverse appliqué designs are universal. Despite minor variations, these designs are easily recognized and have been given names and, sometimes, symbolic meaning by small tribal groups. This leads to confusion in identifying designs, because there are no absolute truths. Only on the snailhouses, the star, and the elephant's foot is there widespread agreement. For many, the star is basic, and all the variations are still stars. For others, the addition of corner "arrows" converts the star to a spiderweb. A row of triangles on a border may represent mountains, shark's teeth, or simply a convenient shape to frame the stitchery. Symbolism, too, is an individual matter. To one, the snailhouse may symbolize eternal life, to another family unity, and to yet another motherhood, simply because it was Mother's favorite pattern.

The inherent confusion of folk legend, coupled with the poetic license of American interpreters, makes any definitive statements regarding symbolism impossible. By our repeated interest and our leading questions, we may be creating imagery that has little or no foundation historically. A newcomer to the art form must accept the inconsistencies with understanding and a smile. The beauty of the designs and the satisfaction derived from their making should be sufficient to encourage widespread recognition and appreciation.

However, nomenclature *is* essential in talking about the designs in this book. In the few instances that a design name exists that is virtually universal among Hmong women of all ages and locations, the name will appear in italics, such as *Snailhouse*. Original names, assigned to other complete designs or portions of designs, will appear in standard type. These names are usually suggested by the similarity of the design to a recognizable object, and they may in a few cases be the names some Hmong women would have used. The use of italics for traditional design names and standard type for new design names will appear throughout the book.

Pa ndau appliqué

The term *pa ndau appliqué* describes the specific craft that combines geometric cutting, reverse appliqué, occasional embellishment with embroidery or appliqué, and the appliquéd borders that complete the large pieces. In this book, the techniques are categorized so that novices can undertake a project with satisfactory results. The exploration of pa ndau appliqué offers the American needle artist an opportunity to refine her appliqué skills, to develop a keen eye, and to explore and experience the joy of geometric paper cutting. The challenge is intense, the rewards are undeniable. Come join in the fun!

"Isn't this a mola?"

Needle artists new to pa ndau often confuse the Hmong stitchery with the mola, a type of reverse appliqué created by the San Blas Indians. In both pa ndau appliqué and molas, the design consists of channels of background fabric that show through cuts in an overlay fabric. There the similarity ends.

The major differences are in the impact of the art and the cutting procedures. Molas are mainly pictorial in nature, while pa ndau appliqué designs are geometric — either snowflake-like or as a single motif repeated over the entire design. For pa ndau appliqué, the design is generally precut into a multifolded overlay before the layers are assembled, establishing lines of symmetry and a near-perfect geometric pattern. For a mola, the layers are assembled first, a design of an object or scene is sketched on the fabric, and then the design is cut. In a mola there is balance, but rarely true symmetry.

A lesser distinction between the two is that for the mola, the background is usually multicolored, whereas for the pa ndau appliqué, the background is rarely multicolored.

Yet another difference between these two graphic folk arts is that, while molas originated in Panama, pa ndau comes to us from a mountain tribe of Indochina. It is fascinating that these two unmistakably similar folk arts should develop in two different areas of the world.

Finally, because of its similarity to paper snowflake cutting, pa ndau appliqué is much more adaptable than molas to the skills of the American needle artist. Virtually everyone who has passed through the American school system has folded squares of paper, snipped into the edges, then unfolded the paper to discover a delightful geometric "snowflake." Now, with pa ndau appliqué, you can translate your elementary school paper cutting into exciting textile art!

1   Materials and Preparation

Pa ndau appliqué is a simple craft to learn. But, as for any craft, you must first acquire the proper equipment, prepare your fabric, and understand the basic construction techniques.

Supplies

- Sheets of typing paper cut into 8½″ squares
- Index cards or clear plastic for templates (optional)
- Circle stencil for circles up to 1½″ in diameter, with quadrant markings (art supply store)
- Scissors for paper cutting
- Scissors for fabric: large ones for fabric cutting and 4″ embroidery scissors for fine work
- Clear plastic ruler with $\frac{1}{16}$″ markings
- Sewing and knitting gauge (a metal 6″ ruler with a sliding indicator — see Templates and Tools, Unit V)
- Fabric-marking utensils for light and dark fabrics
- Pins, thimble, and other standard sewing supplies
- Needles: short needles for appliqué (number 10 betweens) and long, slender needles for basting (number 7 betweens)
- Fabrics: tightly woven 100 percent cotton. Polyester blends are not recommended due to their tendency to fray.

Note: The two types of needles will increase your efficiency. Use the short needle for appliqué, worked one stitch at a time. For basting, use the long needle so that you can take several stitches at a time, leaving large spaces between them.

In choosing fabrics, work only with cotton at first. When you gain experience, you can experiment with unconventional fabrics to achieve a designer effect.

Finally, the list of supplies must include patience and self-forgiveness, because even an appliqué expert may meet an unwelcome challenge in pa ndau snailhouses!

Three-part fabric preparation

If you plan to wash your finished pa ndau piece, carefully color-test, preshrink, and iron the fabrics before you begin cutting and stitching. *Color-testing* means to remove residual dye that might bleed onto the other fabrics during washing. Rinse the fabrics in the sink, or use the washing machine; in either case, rinse the fabrics in reasonably hot water until the water is absolutely clear. *Preshrink* the fabrics using the same washer and dryer settings that will be used to launder the finished product. Then *iron* the fabrics if they are only slightly wrinkled after machine drying. If they are badly crumpled and require excessive pressure and steaming, do not use the fabrics for pa ndau appliqué; you will not want to struggle with the piece after every washing.

If the piece is never to be washed, you may elect not to prewash the fabric. This may be the case for polished cottons or for designer-style pieces with unconventional fabrics and embellishment. The foundation layer fabric is often left unwashed because the manufacturer's finish provides a desirable firmness.

The three layers of pa ndau appliqué

In traditional appliqué, a design is laid on and stitched to a background layer. The design itself is the *appliqué*. In reverse appliqué, the top fabric is laid over the background fabric and the design is cut out of the top piece. *What appears to be the design is actually the lower layer showing through the cut-out portions of the top layer.* In true quilting, the two layers that make the design are called the quilt top, whether they are appliquéd or reverse appliquéd.

To clarify this concept for pa ndau appliqué, the term *overlay* will refer to the piece of fabric into which the design will be cut. The *background* layer will refer to the fabric that shows through the overlay. Hmong needle artists do not use more than one layer of background,

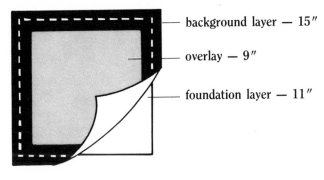

background layer — 15"

overlay — 9"

foundation layer — 11"

Recommended sizes

nor do they piece the background. Therefore, the design is usually only one color in traditional pa ndau. Exceptions are rare.

The third layer in pa ndau appliqué is the *foundation layer*. As the bottom layer, it provides stability to the piece, which is as essential to the stitching process as it is to the finished product. The foundation layer can be a square of plain white or printed fabric. The appliqué stitches will show on the foundation, but if the knots are neatly tied or pulled between the layers as in quilting, the back can be almost as fascinating as the front. If you feel the need to conceal your stitches on the back, simply add a lining or backing to the foundation square before you finish the edges, then tack it in a few spots as needed.

Examination of a large collection of pa ndau appliqué will reveal variations in the basic three layers. The foundation layer is sometimes omitted; whether this is by choice or due to a scarcity of supplies is not known. You may choose to omit the foundation layer, but only if the

design is simple and your skills are refined. Rarely, one might find a two- or three-color background in one design. This is so uncommon that it is likely to be a unique expression by an innovative needle artist, or perhaps an Americanization of the technique. If it were historically authentic, it would probably be far more prevalent. Feel free to experiment with multifabric backgrounds once you have mastered the basic skills.

Pa ndau pieces are commonly finished by hemming. For a simple piece, the background is cut with an allowance for a turned hem. In this case, the foundation should be cut in the exact size of the finished piece so that the hem can be turned along the cut edge of the foundation.

Note: Workable sizes for the designs in this book are a 9" overlay, a 15" background, and an 11" foundation. For smaller pieces, you may select one of the simpler designs. Larger squares may require a combination of designs, elaborate corner treatments, or generous use of appliqué or embroidery and elaborate borders.

2 Folding and Cutting

Designs and motifs

In American quilting, one block represents one pattern — a recognizable and identifiable configuration of shapes. In pa ndau appliqué pieces, the overall design is created by a combination of elements or motifs. Because there are so many motifs from which to choose, the possibilities for designs are virtually limitless. This encourages individualism and creativity, and at the same time plays havoc with any attempts to name or categorize pa ndau appliqué designs. Throughout this book, the term *design* will be used to describe the overall effect, while the term *motif* will refer to the individual elements of the design.

In many cases, one name can refer to both a motif and a full design. When the name is used to indicate a design, it will appear as a title — for instance, Ram's Head. When the discussion is about the motif, the word will appear in lower case, as ram's head. Remember, too, that italics indicate an authentic Hmong design, such as *Snailhouses*.

Don't let this boggle your mind — the word game soon will become routine.

Basic folds

These six folds are the bases for all pa ndau designs. To memorize them, practice them on squares of paper. *Note:* Folds indicated by circled numbers are made only temporarily.

Square. Fold the overlay along the vertical and horizontal axes. The center of the overlay then lies in the lower left-hand corner.

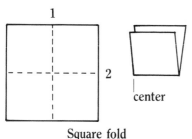

Square fold

Snailhouses. Fold along both diagonal axes. The center of the overlay then lies toward you and is opposite the cut edges. Temporary fold number 3 marks the vertical-horizontal (V/H) lines. Folds 4 and 5 mark the midpoints from the center to the corners on the diagonal folds.

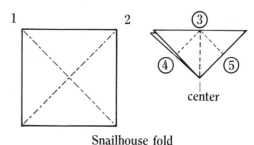

Snailhouse fold

Star. First, fold according to the square fold. Then fold along the diagonal.

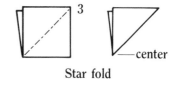

Star fold

Envelope — four-step cutting. Make a square fold to locate the center of the square. Unfold the paper, then fold each corner inward to the center so that the four quadrants are divided diagonally.

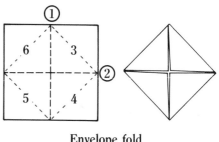

Envelope fold
(four-step cutting)

Envelope — two-step cutting. Fold the upper half of the square down along the horizontal line. Fold the two lower corners up and in toward the center.

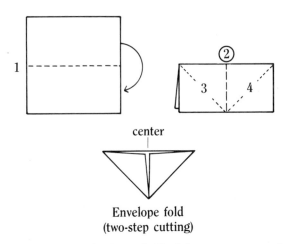

Envelope fold
(two-step cutting)

Pinwheel. Fold the lower half of the square upward along the horizontal line. Then bring the right and left sections of the horizontal fold together along the vertical line.

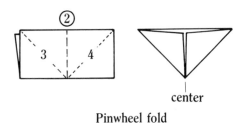

Pinwheel fold

Preparation for cutting

Before you cut your overlay, it must be accurately folded, then basted to keep the folds in place while you cut. All overlays are folded according to one of the six basic methods. Crease the folds with your thumbnail or fingertips, matching the edges precisely. Failure to do this accurately will result in a lopsided design. Now baste the folded overlay along all of the edges, and randomly over the rest of the piece.

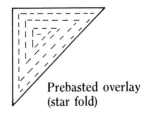

Prebasted overlay
(star fold)

The term *prebaste* will hereafter refer to the basting of the folded overlay prior to cutting. The amount of prebasting required depends on the quality of the fabric and the intricacy of the design. For example, a simple star design on tightly woven fabric will need prebasting only along the edges, with a few stitches in the center of the triangle. More complex designs may require basting stitches in rows ½″ apart. Snailhouses always require extensive prebasting.

Hmong needle artists usually cut overlays without marking the design. At most, they use their thumbnails to draw a straight line or trace around a coin, spool, or button for a circular pattern. An expert can achieve remarkable accuracy with these crude techniques. As a newcomer to pa ndau appliqué, you will be delighted to discover that you can make just a few dots and dashes on the prebasted overlay according to the specific instructions for a design and achieve remarkable precision. If you record the dimensions between the markings by making templates, you will be able to cut a series of reproductions in seconds. As you proceed, you'll find that making templates from index cards is worth the few extra minutes of time and effort. (See Unit V, Chapter 2.)

Precutting

In only a few instances, such as the snailhouse motif, is a complete outline cut into the prebasted overlay. In the majority of designs, only a hint of the individual motifs is snipped into the edges of the folded overlay; the remaining cutting is done in stages after the overlay has been basted to the background and foundation. Cutting done to the prebasted overlay is called *precutting*, whether it completely or only partially cuts the design.

Cutting a folded overlay rather than a flat piece of fabric has two advantages. First, the time spent marking and cutting the design is drastically reduced. More important, however, is the ability to create a uniform design. Folding establishes the lines of symmetry, and all cuts are based upon the distance from the center or from the outer edge. The intrinsic beauty of this method is taught to youngsters when they learn to cut snowflakes from paper. No matter how the paper is folded and cut, a beautiful design is created — success is automatic and almost guaranteed. Pa ndau appliqué offers the same thrill on a more sophisticated level.

For precutting, good scissors are essential. They need not be larger than 4″ embroidery scissors, but they must have sharp points. One popular brand promises to glide through ten layers of fabrics and, fortunately, the advertisement is correct. If your scissors cannot manage so many layers, or if you are using fabric other than broadcloth-weight cotton, you may have to use a two-step cutting process, even for a simple design.

For two-step cutting, you must interrupt the folding process halfway, and mark and cut the two halves individually. Often, it is the intricacy of the design rather than the weight of the fabric that necessitates two-step cutting. In general, snailhouses are cut in two steps so that no more than four layers of fabric are cut at one time. (See Basic Snailhouse for more detailed instructions and diagrams.) Many designs require four-step cutting.

Stacking and basting the layers

The quartering and centering technique used by quilters to properly align the quilt top, batting, and backing is useful for pa ndau appliqué, as well. Fold the background in half horizontally and then in half vertically so that it is neatly quartered. Gently crease the folds, then lay open the square with its right side facing down. In the same way, quarter the foundation layer, crease it, open it, and place it right side up on the background so that the quarter lines match. Pin the squares together along the four sides as close to the edge of the foundation as possible. Turn the piece over so the background is facing up.

When you have completed the precutting, carefully remove the basting and unfold the overlay. Be extremely careful with intricate designs to prevent fraying. Align

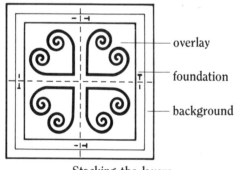

overlay

foundation

background

Stacking the layers

the foldlines of the overlay with the foldlines of the background. The overlay should lie neatly within the pins, in the center of the background. The three layers are now stacked and ready for *foundation basting*. This basting step secures the stacked layers together for stitching. Basically, the foundation basting should lie along

Foundation basting

both the horizontal and vertical axes and the two diagonal axes. For designs such as stars, take one basting stitch between each pair of cuts. For snailhouses, generous basting should lie along the spirals. The more complex the design, the more foundation basting you will need, but you should take care to place your stitches where they will not interfere with tucking under the seam allowances. Finally, baste around the outer edge of the overlay. Either fold under and baste or encase the edges of the background with masking tape to eliminate any fraying as you work.

Postcutting and symmetry

If the precutting provides only a partial design, the major portion of the design is cut after the foundation basting has been completed. This is the *postcutting* and is accomplished in many steps, with only an inch or two cut and stitched at a time. The amount of cutting and stitching undertaken at one time is designated as a *segment*.

Postcutting requires visual estimation and can go awry even if the precutting is impeccable. The critical factor is the establishment of lines of symmetry. If these lines are not already obvious as the vertical/horizontal (V/H) foldlines, mark them with a water-erasable pen. Additional lines may be required for a particular design, but the basic lines of symmetry are as follows:

Vertical: This line runs up and down the center of the square and divides the piece into right and left halves.

Horizontal: This line runs side to side through the center of the square and divides the piece into top and bottom halves.

Right diagonal: This line connects the upper right corner to the lower left corner and divides the square into two triangles — the upper left triangle and the lower right triangle. To mark a right diagonal, begin at the right and draw down.

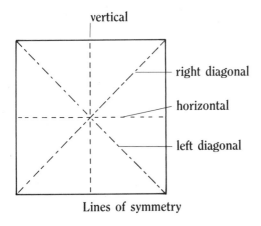

vertical

right diagonal

horizontal

left diagonal

Lines of symmetry

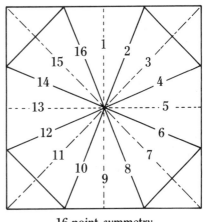

16-point symmetry

Left diagonal: This line connects the upper left corner to the lower right corner and divides the square into the upper right triangle and the lower left triangle. To mark it, begin at the left and draw down.

When both the horizontal and vertical lines of symmetry are present in a design, the square is divided into four quadrants — the upper right, lower right, lower left and upper left. When both diagonal lines of symmetry are used, the square is divided into four equal triangles — the upper, lower, right, and left. When all four lines of symmetry are used in a design, the center is divided into eight equal parts. The design then has *eight-point* symmetry.

Two additional forms of symmetry are used in pa ndau appliqué. The first is dubbed *sixteen-point* symmetry. Based upon eight-point symmetry, it includes four additional lines, drawn as follows:

1 Draw a 2″ square and find the center by drawing the two diagonals. The intersection of the lines is the center.
2 Use a compass to determine **r**, the distance from the center to any corner of the square.

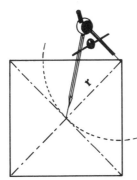

Mark off the distance **r** on all four sides (eight markings).

3 Place the compass point at one corner of the square and mark off the distance **r** on the two adjacent sides. Mark two such distances from the other three corners, marking a total of eight points. These eight points define an octagon.
4 Lines that connect opposing corners of the octagon establish a secondary form of eight-point symmetry. The addition of the diagonal, horizontal, and vertical lines creates sixteen equal angles central to the square.

The final form of symmetry is *radial* symmetry, referring to the relationship of a series of points to the center of the design. They all lie on a circle (with an arbitrary radius) that can be drawn from the center of the square. Radial symmetry is present in most pa ndau designs, but is secondary to other more obvious forms of symmetry.

With all lines of symmetry, you may mark the lines or simply imagine them. Before you cut each segment, lightly mark the cutting line with your thumbnail or with a water-erasable marker until you develop the necessary keen eye. *The cutting line is actually the midline of a channel of background fabric that will appear as the seam allowances are turned under and stitched.*

To postcut, slip one point of the embroidery scissors between the overlay and the background through one of the precut slits. Carefully cut along the marked line. Clip corners and seam allowances as required by the design without disturbing the foundation basting. Turn the fabric under and secure with appliqué stitches. This will form a channel of background fabric. It is the channel that creates the design.

One of the most sophisticated forms of postcutting involves zigzag-cutting on one side of the channel. This

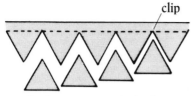

Cutting a saw-toothed edge

is usually done by keen estimation, but you may certainly mark off guidelines until you feel secure. Always stitch the straight side before zigzag-cutting so that the overlay is securely in position. Then cut away a row of triangles from the free side of the overlay. Clip the corners, turn under the seam allowances, and stitch. This treatment creates a lovely saw-toothed finish for a square. When it is used in a simplified snailhouse, it is sometimes called *dragon's tail.*

Decorative and foundation cutting

After all of the precut channel stitching on the entire piece has been completed, you may add decorative cutting to the foundation-basted overlay. This cutting technique is most frequently used to add corner or center motifs, or occasionally to cut an asymmetrical motif. Decorative cutting is not marked or cut on the folded overlay, and it requires considerable expertise. To do decorative cutting, separate the overlay from the background by pinching the overlay at the point desired for the incision. Snip a thread or two so that you are able to insert the point of the scissors, then cut as required for the design. Such cutting is tedious and risky and usually is limited to center and corner designs. On the other hand, some of the most intriguing designs are cut *entirely* by this method, and are designated as completely *foundation cut. Froglegs* and *Cucumber Seeds* are two popular examples. Obviously, they are not for the beginner! Decorative cutting and foundation cutting can be used to create a simple corner motif or an intricate allover design. In either case, the need for skill and patience is as great as the risks involved.

3 The Appliqué Stitch

Pa ndau appliqué requires mastery of the appliqué stitch, a tiny, visible stitch that lies perpendicular to the folded edge of the appliqué. Using a practice piece of fabric, follow these steps to refine your technique.

1 Iron under a narrow seam allowance on one piece of fabric and pin or baste it to a second, larger piece. The top fabric represents the overlay (appliqué) and the larger piece represents the background. The folded edge will be stitched.
2 Using a knotted single thread, insert the needle from the back of the larger piece so that the needle comes to the surface *through* the appliqué, just a thread or two from the folded edge.

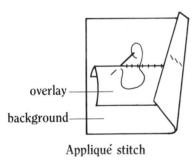

overlay
background

Appliqué stitch

3 Insert the needle in the background layer, right next to the folded edge of the appliqué. How carefully you do this will determine how straight your stitches will be and whether they will all be the same size.
4 Direct the needle diagonally to the left on the underside of the fabrics and bring the needle point to the surface through the appliqué, $\frac{1}{16}''$ away from the first stitch. Pull the needle to the top.
5 Repeat steps three and four, striving for consistency in stitch length and the distance between the stitches. On the front, the appliqué stitches will be tiny threads crossing perpendicular to the folded edge and parallel to one another, and on the back, the stitches will form a row of diagonal threads.

To secure corners and points, the appliqué stitch is strong and attractive when sewn as follows:

Corners

1 Clip the seam allowance of the overlay to within a thread or two of the corner foldline. For greatest precision and minimal fraying, always hold the scissors so that the clip lies on the true diagonal of the corner.
2 Use the point of the needle to tuck under the seam allowance. Stitch, judging the distance between the stitches carefully, so that they are nicely spaced at the corner. If the overlay fabric is a tight weave, you will be able to place a stitch exactly in the corner. *On looser weaves or off-grain cuts, it may be safer to place a stitch slightly to each side of the corner so that the stitching itself does not cause fraying.*

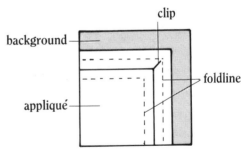

clip

background

foldline

appliqué

Clip the corners to within two or three threads of the foldline.

Points

1 Tuck under the seam allowance on the first side, using the needle. Stitch along the first side of the point, stopping approximately $\frac{1}{4}''$ from the point.
2 Use the needle to tuck under the seam allowance on the second side.

15

3 Finish stitching the first side, tucking all seam allowances well beneath the folded edge, so that only one folded layer of fabric is caught in the stitches.

4 Place stitches neatly on each side of the point and make one diagonal stitch *exactly* at the point.

In pa ndau appliqué, the seam allowance is tucked under one segment at a time as the piece is stitched, and the design appears as the background is exposed. When the second side of each cut is stitched, a *channel* of background appears. In pa ndau appliqué, the overall design is a collection of channels, hopefully all the same width. For simple designs in the scale used in this book, the width of a channel is usually $\frac{3}{16}''$.

The fabric between two channels is a *strip*, usually the same width as the channel. You may wish to increase the width of the channels. Particularly with snailhouses, Hmong women tuck under a far greater proportion of the fabric. Experts tuck under such a wide seam allowance that the remaining strip almost looks like cording. A keen eye is a great asset, but those who lack it can compensate with practice and rapt attention — thank goodness!

In pa ndau appliqué, stitching is usually begun at the center of the design. Two rounds of stitching are required for each channel. They are designated as round 1 and round 2.

4 Finishing and Design Correction

Finishing

The way in which you finish a piece can add to the overall design. Stitch the outer edge of the overlay according to one of the suggested finishes. (See Unit IV, Chapter 1.) Examine the completed piece and determine whether it would be improved with embellishments, considering the balance of design and the balance of color. Embellishments may be embroidery, appliqué, or reverse appliqué (IV: Chapter 2).

To improve the design

If the center of your design is too dense and the corners sparse, add corner embellishments. If the design is diagonal, it will appear more balanced with the addition of embroidery at all corners and along the vertical and horizontal axes.

If there is a boring space at the center, fill it.

If the design is angular and you prefer a touch of whimsy, add a few single spirals.

If the design seems too plain, add rickrack motifs at the north, south, east, and west points.

If the design seems too predictable, turn the finished piece so that it lies diagonally and use it that way.

To improve the balance of color

If there appears to be too much of the overlay color and too little of the background, use reverse appliqué in the corners and along the sides to increase the proportion of the background color.

If the colors vibrate (red and green in equal amounts create this effect), leave a wide border of the background and embellish the overlay with small appliqués in the border color. This alters the proportion of one color to the other.

If the piece lacks vitality, enhance it with appliqué or embroidery in colors that do not already appear in the piece.

Whatever embellishments you choose, remember that the use of color may create secondary designs that can overwhelm the basic pattern instead of improving it. Appliqué is the safest form of embellishment because you can lay the appliqués on the pa ndau piece and judge their impact. Decorative cutting, on the other hand, cannot be tested. And a bad decision is irreversible.

When you are satisfied with the finished piece, remove all basting and autograph the foundation in the lower right-hand corner. Then appliqué the completed piece onto a vest, tote bag, or pillow; hem the edges and use the appliqué as it is, or use it as a unit in a larger piece.

5 The Floor Plan for Success

In order to understand the concept of geometric paper cutting and to master the stitching techniques, study these seven exercises in the order in which they are listed.

1 Basic folds. Learn to execute all six from memory.
2 Symmetry. Develop a comprehension of the forms of symmetry by folding squares of paper and making random cuts along the folds. Try straight cuts perpendicular to the fold and along the diagonals, and cut snailhouses. (See Unit II.) Open each square and analyze the results. Learn to predict the results before you cut. If you have difficulty with this, draw an imaginary cut on the folded paper and study its orientation on the flat square.
3 Star design. Begin in-depth examination of the star design by cutting all of the variations on paper. Cut and stitch a three-channel star with arrows to gain experience with eight-point symmetry, straight channel stitching, points, and corners.
4 Snailhouses. Begin to master snailhouses. This will require a great deal of practice cutting on both paper and fabric. Learn to predict the proper folding and cutting in order to position pairs of snailhouses on all lines of symmetry. Practice stitching.
5 Pa ndau appliqué designs. Learn to analyze pa ndau appliqué designs by studying the photographs of the designs and writing your own instructions for folding and cutting. Watch for alternate ways to create a design. Consider how you would undertake two-part cutting if it should be necessary. Finally, mark and cut all of the variations included in Unit III: Chapter 3 from squares of paper.
6 Stitching order. Analyze the designs in terms of logical stitching order.
7 Creating original designs. Create original pa ndau appliqué by folding a dozen or more squares of paper in a variety of symmetries and cutting to your heart's content. As you examine each cut design, analyze the spacing of the motifs and consider how you could improve the overall design.

The joys of pa ndau appliqué — both cutting and stitching — are indescribable. Even if you never sew a stitch, experimenting with paper cutting is therapeutic because of its built-in precision. Soon you'll be eager to try again, to use a complex fold, or to add a secondary design. Snip, snip, snip — suddenly dragon's tails cover the table top and spill onto the floor.

The actual stitching brings a quieter sense of fulfillment. You may find, as I have, that pa ndau appliqué is even more demanding, fulfilling, and awe-inspiring than American patchwork and quilting. Through pa ndau appliqué, you will discover creation, color, satisfaction, challenge, mental exercise, therapy, excitement . . . peace.

1 **Basic Star Motif**

Certain design elements of pa ndau appliqué are so prominent and easily recognized that they dominate the overall appearance of a piece. These are the *primary motifs*. The two most important primary motifs are the star and snailhouses, or snailhouse pair. If a set of four snailhouse pairs is decorated with rings, a new primary motif is formed — the elephant's foot. Two other motifs, the ram's head and the heart, combine straight channels with spirals. "Ram's head" is a newly assigned name, but "heart" is recognized by the Hmong. These five primary motifs are the bases for the majority of pa ndau appliqué designs.

Any needle artist who wishes to master pa ndau appliqué must understand the cutting procedures and the stitching techniques of these basic motifs.

This basic motif is the best for beginners. The cutting is simple, and it will give you valuable stitching experience before you move on to the more difficult spiral motifs.

Fold an 8½"-square overlay according to the instructions for the star. (See Unit I, Chapter 2.) Prebaste. With a water-erasable pen, mark off points 2", 2½", and 3" from the center on the left-hand fold (vertical/horizontal axes) and points 2", 2½", 3", and 3½" on the diagonal fold. The outermost marking on the diagonal fold indicates the position of the corner arrows. Cut a ³⁄₁₆" snip at each marking, paying careful attention to the angle of the scissors. *On the diagonal fold, the cuts*

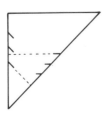

For stars, cut perpendicular to the opposite fold.

must be made perpendicular to the vertical/horizontal fold. On the vertical/horizontal fold, the cuts must be made perpendicular to the diagonal fold. Remove the prebasting. (Hereafter, the term vertical/horizontal fold will be abbreviated as V/H fold.)

Open the overlay and stack the foundation, background, and overlay by the quartering and centering method (see Unit I for dimensions and techniques). Foundation baste the layers along the V/H and diagonal axes, using caution not to baste down any of the seam allowances. The V/H and diagonal folds determine eight-point symmetry. Precise marking and cutting along

16th line

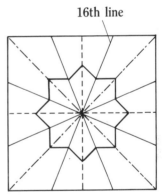

Proper symmetry for basic star

these folds ensures that the eight points of the star design will be evenly spaced. However, because the star has sixteen sides, the marking needs additional refinement.

With your thumbnail, mark the line that divides the angle at the center in half. This line *bisects* the angle and establishes the points at which the sides of the star meet. This line and the other four like it are the secondary lines of eight-point symmetry. We shall call them sixteenth lines.

Referring to the outline of the star in the diagram, use your thumbnail to mark the cutting lines for the first two segments; for the star, one segment is one side of the star point. Two segments join star point to star point. Failure to neatly join the sides of the star on a sixteenth line will result in a lopsided star. Clip the seam allowance at the corner between the two segments. The clip must lie on the sixteenth line.

Stitch the first round counterclockwise, beginning at the top of the star with the innermost channel. Rotate the fabric so that the first side to be stitched lies horizontal in your hands, with the clipped corner at the left and the point of the star on the right. Use the needle point to tuck under the seam allowance at the clip and hold the fabric in place with your left hand. Move the needle to the right and shift your left thumb slightly so that the entire fold is secured.

Note: Tucking under the seam allowances with the needle point is accurate and efficient, and it also reduces wear and tear on fragile edges. Your success with this method depends upon the angle at which you hold the needle. It should be 45 degrees *up* from the horizontal fold of the overlay and approximately 45 degrees *out* from the background. Belief in the adage practice makes perfect also helps.

Holding under the seam allowance with your left hand, stitch the side of the first star point, ending at the clipped corner (see Appliqué Stitch). Rotate the fabric so that the next segment lies horizontal in your hands. Beginning at the star point, which lies at the left, tuck under the seam allowance. Then stitch the second segment from the clipped corner toward the point.

A few stitches from the point, stop stitching and cut the next two segments so that the seam allowances at the corner are completely free. Use the needle to tuck under the seam allowances, forming a crisp point, and stitch to the corner (see Appliqué Stitch). Continue to cut and stitch segments until the first round is completed. Always rotate the fabric so that stitching can be done at a comfortable angle.

For the second round of stitching, begin at the bottom and stitch in a clockwise direction. The directional change from counterclockwise to clockwise for the first and second rounds of each channel of the star orients the stitching so that the seam allowances are always folded toward your body, making the stitching easier and more uniform.

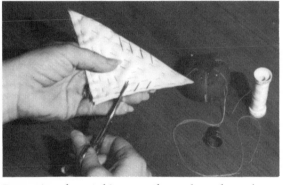

Precutting the markings on the prebasted overlay

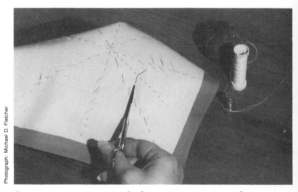

Cut two segments of the star, turning the corner precisely on a sixteenth line.

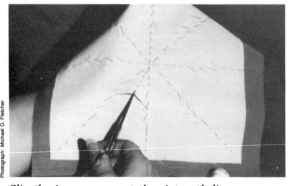

Clip the inner corner at the sixteenth line.

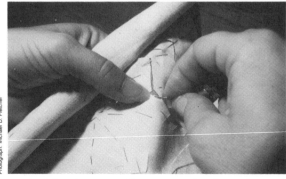

Tuck under the seam allowance at the clip and secure it with your left thumb.

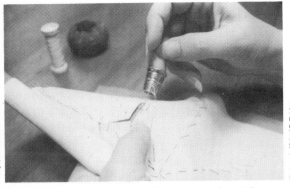

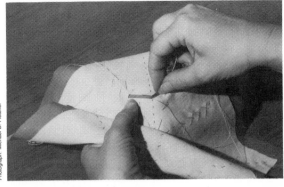

As you stitch, hold the seam allowance under with your left hand.

Stitching the second segment

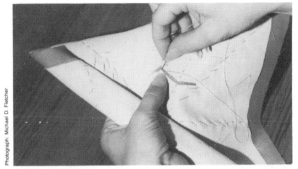

Use the needle point to turn under the seam allowance at the corner.

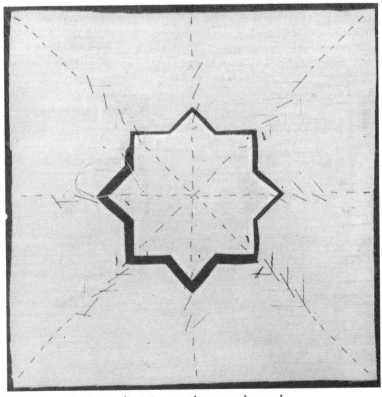

Stitch in a clockwise direction on the second round.

Repeat this procedure, working out to each subsequent channel. Stitch the four corner arrows by making five corner clips and one folded point for each arrow. Although your first corners and points may be slightly less than perfect, you'll quickly improve and feel encouraged as the second round of stitching on the first channel exposes the background fabric and the design appears. By the third channel, the basics will be second nature. And fortunately, the corners are done last when you have achieved a certain amount of expertise.

Once you've mastered these basics, you can feel proud of your accomplishment — you now can stitch any star, no matter how many channels or what the corner motifs.

The specifications for the basic star are repeated here in the format that will be used for all star designs throughout the book. Read them carefully, referring to the photographs and general instructions as necessary, so that you feel comfortable with the terminology and techniques.

Basic Star

Fold	Star.
Marking	*V/H fold:* 2″, 2½″, and 3″ from the center of the overlay.
	Eight-point fold: 2″, 2½″, 3″, and 3½″ from the center of the overlay.
Precutting	Cut a ³⁄₁₆″ snip at all seven markings.
Postcutting	After foundation basting, cut the three channels for the star in segments. One precut will remain for the corner arrows.
Finish	Simple (see Finishes).
Embellishment	Center diamonds (see Embellishments).

Basic Star Motif

2 Basic Snailhouse Motif

The snailhouse is such an important motif in pa ndau appliqué that a specific word is used to differentiate the needlework design from the living creature. The snailhouse motif is as difficult as it is important. Detailed instruction and patient practice will bring you the success you desire, and mastery of the snailhouse will enable you to create virtually any other curved design competently.

For the snailhouse, the outer circle is actually drawn onto the prebasted overlay. This is called the *rim*. The center of the spiral is the *core*. Because the entire spiral

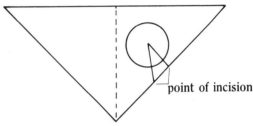

point of incision

Point of incision may vary.

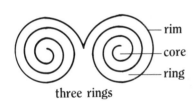

— rim
— core
— ring

three rings

five rings

The depth of the incision affects the appearance of a snailhouse pair.

is actually only one channel, the term *ring* will be used to distinguish segments of the spiral. The initial cut at the fold of the overlay is the *incision*. Two snailhouses that are joined along a line of symmetry are a *snailhouse pair*.

Between the two halves of the snailhouse pair is a V. The point of the V is actually the incision made at the fold of the prebasted overlay. The angle at which the incision is made will greatly affect both the difficulty and the appearance of the snailhouse pair. The angle is determined by two factors: the relationship between the

core and the point of incision, and the distance from the fold to the rim of the circle. The incision may lie in line with the lowest point of the rim, in line with the very center of the circle, or anywhere in between.

The distance between the rim of the circle and the fold affects the incline of the V. The closer the rim is to the fold, the steeper the V is, and the farther the rim is from the fold, the flatter the V is. For uniformity and simplification, the instructions for the individual designs will all specify that the incision be made in line with the center of the circle, and with a distance between the rim and the fold that is proportional to the size of the circle.

The incline of the V affects the difficulty of the snailhouse pair. The steeper the V, the harder it is to stitch. The level of difficulty of a particular snailhouse motif is also determined by the size of the circle and the number of rings it contains. To count the rings, begin at the core and count away from the incision. Two circles, both 1½ ″ in diameter, may differ from an easy three rings to a difficult five rings.

Develop an eye

Using a compass, stencil, or simply tracing around a convenient object, draw a series of circles that are 1 ″ to 1½ ″ in diameter on a piece of paper.

Beginning at the outside of one circle, draw a spiraling line to its center, making no more than three rings. All the rings must be the same width.

23

As you draw, look toward the outer ring and not toward the center of the circle. It is the uniformity of the distance from your pencil to the previously drawn ring that determines the precision of your design. The core will fall into place if all the rings have been uniformly drawn.

Marking and practice cutting

Fold a 4″ square of paper according to the snailhouse fold. (See Unit I, Chapter 2.) Mark an incision point 1″ from the center of the overlay along the right diagonal fold. Hold a ruler perpendicular to the right fold and mark a line ⅝″ long. The point at the end of this line is the center of the circle that forms the rim of the snailhouse. Draw the circle, using your 1″-diameter circle stencil. Position the stencil so that one quadrant marking is lined up with your ⅝″ line, and so that the quadrants cross on your marked center.

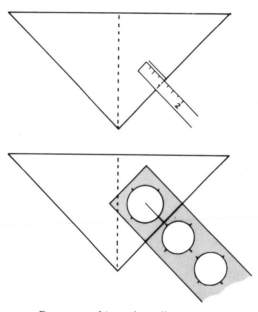

Proper marking of snailhouses

To mark this snailhouse, you used three specifications: First, the distance from the center of the prebasted overlay to the point of incision, a point marked on the fold. Second, the distance from the fold to the center of the circle, marked at the end of a line perpendicular to the fold. And third, the diameter of the circle that becomes the rim of the cut snailhouse, marked with a stencil. Instructions for any design requiring snailhouse pairs will always include these three specifications.

Note: To mark the line perpendicular to the fold, a sewing and knitting gauge is an extremely useful tool. Slide the metal indicator to the required distance (⅝″ in the previous example). Lay the edge of the indicator alongside the fold and mark the point at the end of the ruler. It's that simple.

To cut your snailhouse pair, begin at the point on the fold that lies in line with the center of the circle. This is point C, for core. Cut a gentle curve from point C up to the drawn circle at point R, for rim (see diagram). Cut along the drawn circle to point D, for departure. At D, change the angle of the scissors so that you cut *inside* the drawn line. This is the beginning of the outer ring. Points R and D are not exact but, with practice, you will be able to guess their proper position. Watch

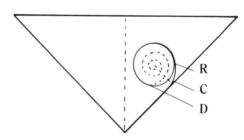

Right-orientation snailhouses

the previously cut edge as you cut the spiral, maintaining as uniform a width as possible. Rotate the center portion of the circle to make cutting easier, and allow the finished spiral to fall away. Cut the spiral all the way to the core.

Open the paper out flat on the table, carefully separating the layers of the snailhouse pairs from the rim toward the center. Lay all of the rings neatly in place and examine your work.

Repeat this process until you can accurately cut a snailhouse of three rings. Then experiment with snailhouses of four or five rings, remembering that it is the angle of the scissors during the cutting *from* point D (that is, the departure from the drawn line) that determines the width of the rings. A gentle departure from the drawn circle will create a spiral of narrow rings, while a sharper angle will result in a smaller number of wider rings.

Right and left orientation

In all of your snailhouse practice cutting, the circle has been marked with the fold on the right. In the opened piece, the V of each snailhouse pair has always pointed toward the center of the square. This is called a right-orientation (RO) snailhouse pair. It is possible to cut snailhouse pairs that have a V pointing outward, but cutting would be difficult if the marking were done on the right fold. Therefore, a different method is required to cut left-orientation snailhouses.

In the snailhouse pair with left orientation (LO), the V points up, or away from the center of the overlay. For this orientation, the marking occurs on the *left-hand fold*. Fold a piece of paper and mark it as you did for the

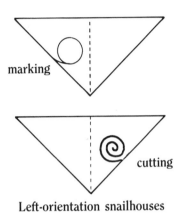

Left-orientation snailhouses

RO snailhouses, but mark on the left-hand fold. Then rotate the paper, keeping the marked side up, so that the marked fold is now on the right. The cutting procedure is identical to that for RO snailhouses, except that the center of the design is lying away from your body. Don't make this seem harder than it really is. The marking is done with the fold on the left. For cutting, the fold is turned until it is on the right, and the center of the square points *away*.

You will master the proper terminology more quickly if you remember this: In RO snailhouses, the V is *right-side* up. Mark on the *right* fold. For LO, the V is *wrong* (upside-down), so mark on the *wrong* side (left). These rules apply for right-handed people only. Memorize the rules as stated so that the key words are linked. Soon you will be able to follow all pa ndau appliqué directions without hesitation or error.

Left-handed needle workers are usually adept at translating right-handed instructions for their own needs. But for something as complex as snailhouse orientation, the instructions are specific. The terms right and left orientation must remain unchanged so that general instructions can be used by both right- and left-handed craftsmen. If you are left-handed, you will mark a RO

snailhouse on the left-hand fold and, with special lefty scissors, cut upward and to the right with the center of the overlay lying toward your body. For a LO snailhouse, mark the right-hand fold, and rotate the fabric so that the fold is on the left, ready for cutting. It may be helpful at first to write out these left-handed orientation instructions on an index card and move them from page to page for reference as you progress from design to design.

Right-handed people should always cut counterclockwise and left-handers should cut clockwise, regardless of the orientation of the snailhouse pairs.

Two-step marking and cutting

The majority of snailhouse designs have four snail-house pairs forming a ring in the center. Technically, these designs could be cut in one step using the star fold, but because snailhouses require such precise cutting, a two-step process is necessary. This process reduces the number of layers from the usual eight in star designs to a more workable four. The first and second steps are identical for any specific motif, and this variation in technique does not affect the property of orientation.

To develop an understanding of two-step snailhouse marking, fold an 8½″ square of paper according to the snailhouse fold. Mark a RO snailhouse (the incision lies 2¼″ from the center of the overlay; the center of the circle lies 1″ from the right fold; the circle is 1¼″ in diameter). Turn over the triangularly folded piece so

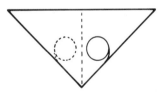

Two-step marking of snailhouses

that what was the back faces you and the center is still toward you. Mark a second RO snailhouse on *this* side of the paper. Both the front and back of the triangle are identically marked. Cut the snailhouses. Open the paper and observe the results.

Fold a second square of paper. Mark and cut LO snailhouses using the same specifications that were used to cut the first sample. Mark these two paper designs RO and LO respectively. Commit this concept to memory by cutting paper squares until you feel confident of both the terminology and your own ability.

Stitching snailhouses

Cut an 8½″ square of practice fabric. Fold it according to snailhouse instructions and prebaste thoroughly. Mark two RO snailhouses using the same specifications that were used for paper cutting in the previous section. Cut no more than three rings. Remove the prebasting, open the overlay, and stack and baste the layers according to the basic instructions.

The foundation basting for simple designs and stars is easily accomplished and requires minimal effort. But for snailhouse pairs, the quality of your finished piece depends largely on this step. Begin basting at the V, and make tiny basting stitches down the center of the spiraling rings to the core of the snailhouse. Rotate the

curves in the diagram. *Concave* means hollow or rounded inward. Trace the concave curves in the diagram. In the star design, both the first and second rounds of a channel use identical stitching techniques and are alike in difficulty. But the two rounds of the snailhouse spiral are extremely different, for one is concave and one is convex.

Making a tiny clip at the V, begin stitching at point A, indicated on the diagram. Tuck under the seam allowance with the needle point and hold the fold in place securely with your left thumb. The seam allowance should be approximately one-fourth of the width of the cut ring. Fortunately, the first few stitches are along a fairly straight fold. Sew along the convex curve, tucking under the seam allowance just ahead of the stitching,

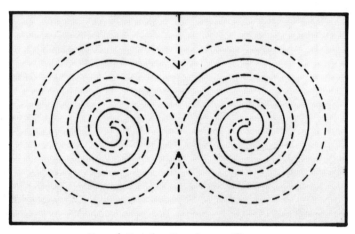

Foundation basting for snailhouses

fabric as you baste so that you are always working at a comfortable angle. Upon completion of the first snailhouse, break the thread and baste the second of the pair in the same fashion. Baste all of the pairs, the V/H and diagonal axes, and the outer edge.

After all of the new terminology needed to clarify the marking of snailhouses, it seems there couldn't be any left. But there are two more terms that are important to understand for stitching. They are concave and convex. *Convex* means bowed outward. Trace the convex

and stitching through to the foundation layer. It will not be possible to tuck or stitch more than ¼″ at a time. *No clipping is necessary on the convex round of stitching.* Continually rotate the fabric so that you are stitching at a comfortable angle. When you reach the core of the snailhouse — the turning point — fold under the seam allowances to form a neat point and begin stitching the second side of the spiral.

The second side is the concave curve. It is far more difficult, and the seam allowances along this side will

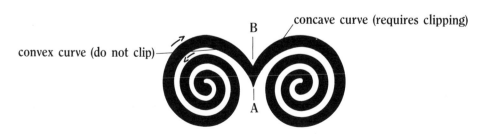

concave curve (requires clipping)

convex curve (do not clip)

B

A

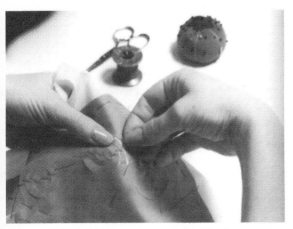

Begin stitching at the bottom of the V, drawing the needle from left to right to tuck under the seam allowance.

Rotate the fabric so that the stitching can be done at a comfortable angle.

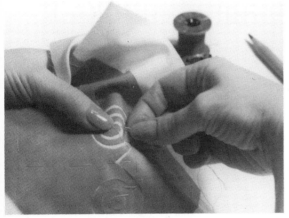

Turn a soft "point" at the core of the spiral and begin stitching the second side of the channel.

Complete one snailhouse before beginning to stitch the second of the pair.

require extensive clipping, especially toward the core. Use caution not to clip too deeply, but clip often enough to avoid unsightly dimples on the curve. When you reach point B in the diagram, turn under a neat point and continue stitching along the concave curve. Always hold the fabric so that the folded seam allowance lies toward your body, and stitch toward the left. For the snailhouse, this means that the fabric will sometimes be rotated counterclockwise and sometimes clockwise. This will

become obvious as you stitch. *Snailhouses are all stitched in this fashion whether they are right or left in orientation.*

Stitch the first pair of snailhouses on your practice fabric. Your primary goal is to learn the difference between convex and concave curves and to experience the stitching of both types. On this first try, the channel will probably narrow and widen several times. For the second snailhouse pair, you may wish to mark a faint dotted line along the foldline of the channel to remove some of the guesswork. Remember, though, that Hmong experts *do not* mark any foldlines. *This is because compensation for slight irregularities in the cutting of the snailhouses can be achieved if you judge the width of the channel as it is exposed rather than the amount of seam allowance that is being turned under.*

Don't give up. By the third snailhouse pair, you should see remarkable improvement. The fourth may be almost acceptable!

Basic Snailhouses*

Fold	Snailhouse.
Two-step marking	Both sides are identical with RO snailhouses. The incision lies $2\frac{5}{8}''$ from the center of the overlay; the center of the circle lies $\frac{7}{8}''$ from the right diagonal fold; the circle is $1\frac{1}{2}''$ in diameter.
Precutting	Completely cut the snailhouses.
Detail	Although the circle is large, the beginner should cut no more than three rings in the snailhouse.
Finish	Simple (see Finishes).
Embellishment	Diamonds (see Embellishments).

*These snailhouses are in right orientation. See the general information for a full explanation of this concept.

Basic Snailhouse Motif

3 Basic Elephant's Foot Motif

The elephant's foot motif is actually nothing more than snailhouse pairs surrounded by rings, but its historical significance as a traditional Hmong pattern lends it distinction and sets it in the ranks of primary motifs. Because snailhouses are now a part of your pa ndau repertoire, the explanation of the elephant's foot motif will be limited to the special techniques related to rings.

A Hmong needle artist would cut the rings largely by guesswork. But for the newcomer to the folk art, guidelines are a welcome aid. The marking requires an unusual folding process, but the resulting security is well worth the effort.

To make the elephant's foot, first fold and prebaste the overlay according to the snailhouse fold. Then fold the overlay along the V/H fold so that you have a star-folded overlay. Run a line of temporary prebasting along

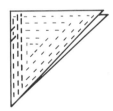

Temporarily prebaste the overlay into a star fold.

the V/H fold. Referring to the specific dimensions for the design at the end of this chapter, mark the placement of the rings with short lines along the V/H fold. Cut *tiny* snips, no more than ⅟₁₆ ″ deep, along the marked lines. These minute perforations in the overlay will be sufficient indication for postcutting of the rings, but it is critical that the snips be minimal, because it is difficult to imagine the proper angle before the snailhouses have been cut. Remove the temporary prebasting, restoring the overlay to the snailhouse fold.

Now mark the rest of the design along the diagonal folds according to the specifications for the design. Com-

pletely cut the snailhouses. Then cut approximately ⅛ ″ snips parallel to the vertical fold at the markings for the rings.

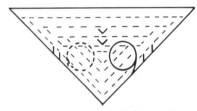

Restore the overlay to the snailhouse fold to complete marking.

Because this design requires a double folding and cutting process, it is considered *complex*. This term refers to the precutting process only, not to the appliqué process. As you gain experience, you may eliminate the temporary prebasting along the V/H fold as you mark and cut measurements for the rings. Ultimately, you may dispense with any marking of the rings along the V/H axes at all! This would switch the process from complex to simple status.

Stitch the snailhouse pairs as explained in Unit II, Chapter 2. Always stitch the snailhouse pairs before you begin stitching the rings.

To postcut and stitch the rings, each segment should be the curve from one point to the next (from diagonal fold to V/H fold) for a total of eight segments in the standard ring. For most designs using an 8½ ″ square overlay, the channel will be ³⁄₁₆ ″ wide. But the exposed area at a point will be approximately ½ ″ wide. As the diagram indicates, this is because, at the point, the width is actually a diagonal measurement. This is not a major issue, but can be a bit puzzling. When stitching, you may find it helpful to clip away the tips of the seam allowances at the points. But remember that the width here will not be the same as the rest of the channel.

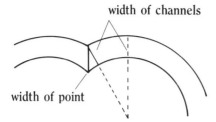

width of channels

width of point

For multiple rings, complete the innermost ring first. *When design specifications indicate the distance between rings or the distance between a ring and the rim of a snailhouse pair, they refer to the distance between the midlines of the two channels.*

Basic Elephant's Foot

Fold	Snailhouse/Star.
Complex marking	Temporarily fold along the V/H axes, basting if necessary (see the basic instructions). On the V/H fold, mark

rings 2¾ ″ and 3¼ ″ from the center of the overlay and snip. Restore to snailhouse fold and proceed with marking.

With RO snailhouses, both sides are identical. The incision lies 2¼ ″ from the center of the overlay; center of the circle lies ⅞ ″ from the right-hand fold; the circle is 1⅜ ″ in diameter.

	Rings: 2¾ ″ and 3¼ ″ from the center of the overlay (see basic instructions).
Precutting	Completely cut the snailhouses. For the rings, cut no more than 1⁄16 ″ to ⅛ ″ snips into the folds.
Postcutting	After the snailhouses have been stitched, cut and stitch the rings, one segment at a time. The rings should lie 3⁄16 ″ apart.
Finish	Simple (see Finishes).
Embellishment	Dog's Foot (see Embellishments).

Basic Elephant's Foot Motif

4 Basic Ram's Head Motif

The ram's head motif combines the spiraling curves of the snailhouse with the exacting points of the star. It requires the skill and precision of an expert.

The parts of the ram's head are the base and the horn, or spiral. The motif can take on different appearances depending upon the length of the base and its distance from the spiral. The size of the spiral and its distance from the fold also play a minor role.

Marking and cutting

To make the rams' heads, use the snailhouse fold. Like the snailhouse pairs, rams' heads can be executed in orientations. In right orientation, the base lies toward the center of the overlay. In left orientation, the base lies away from the center. The specifications for marking include the distance the base lies from the center

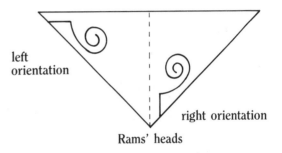

left orientation

right orientation

Rams' heads

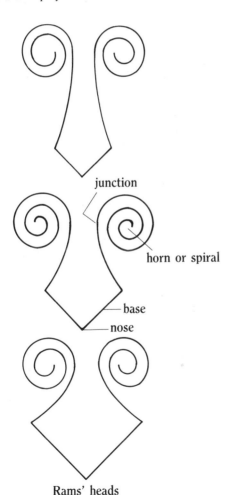

junction

horn or spiral

base

nose

Rams' heads

of the overlay and the length of the base. For right orientation, the base must be drawn and cut exactly parallel to the V/H axes of the overlay. You may choose to fold the prebasted overlay in half, creasing the V/H fold, so that marking can be easily and correctly accomplished. For left orientation, the base lies parallel to the outer edges of the square overlay.

To position the horn, first mark the distance along the fold from the center of the overlay. Then mark the distance from the fold to the center of the circle. And, finally, draw the rim of the circle itself.

Mark on the right-hand fold for a RO ram's head and on the left-hand fold for a LO ram's head. This permits counterclockwise cutting of the spirals, which is easiest for a right-handed needle artist. Left-handed people should mark on the opposite fold for each orientation and cut in a clockwise direction.

No incision is made in the fold alongside the rim of the spiral. Instead, the cutting stems from the inner end

31

of the base, from the interior of the prebasted overlay. The line of cutting that joins the base and the spiral will be fairly straight or severely curved depending upon the relative size of the two and the distance between them. The point at which the line of cutting meets the rim of the spiral is the *junction*. It lies on the imaginary line that joins the center of the circle to the mark on the fold that indicates the specified distance from the center of the overlay.

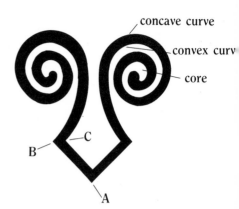

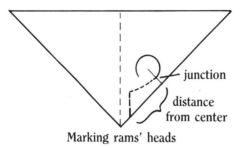

Marking rams' heads

Reverse appliqué

To prevent shifting and distortion that could occur as you appliqué the intricate ram's head motif, baste the layers extensively. Then, to stitch, begin at the nose by making a tiny clip at points A and B as shown in the diagram. Turn under the seam allowance from A to B and stitch. After you execute a precision corner at B, begin to stitch the spiral. This first round of the channel follows a convex curve and does not require clipping. Rotate the piece as you stitch so that you are always stitching at a comfortable angle. At the core, turn a neat

point and begin the concave curve. This round of stitching will require clipping, especially at the core. Corner C will not require clipping. Complete the base and stitch the second horn.

Basic Rams' Heads

Fold	Snailhouse.
Two-step marking	Both sides are identical with RO rams' heads. The base begins ⅜″ from the center of the overlay and is 1¼″ in length. The junction lies on a line 2½″ from the center of the overlay. The center of the circle lies 1″ from the fold. The circle is 1⅛″ in diameter.
Precutting	Completely cut the base of the ram's head and the spirals.
Finish	Channel (see Finishes).

Basic Ram's Head Motif

5 Basic Heart Motif

The heart is symbolic in many cultures, suggesting love, piety, or life itself. But the interpretation of this symbol by the Hmong needle artists is exceptional. The sleek sides of pa ndau hearts curve gently around the two hemispheres of the top, where the channels wind into delightful, spiraling crowns. This motif is no more difficult than the ram's head to stitch. It is because of the technical aspects of marking and cutting that this primary motif has been saved for last.

In snailhouses, the right orientation involves marking on the right-hand fold, cutting is done counterclockwise, and the point of the V lies *toward* the center of the overlay. The same rules apply for elephant's foot and

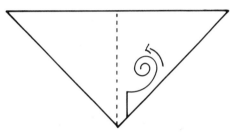

Right-orientation ram's head
(cut in counterclockwise direction)

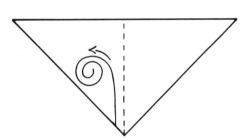

Right-orientation heart (cut in counterclockwise direction)

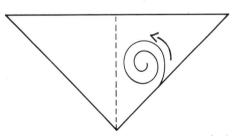

Right-orientation snailhouse (cut in counterclockwise direction)

ram's head. The V, or the base in the case of the ram's head, always points toward the center if marking is done on the right-hand fold. *For the heart, however, if the point is to lie toward the center, the heart must be marked on the left-hand fold.* This is necessary to permit counterclockwise cutting.

For the heart shape, the cutting begins parallel to the V/H foldline and then moves toward the diagonal foldline around the rim of the spiral. For the other RO motifs, when the V or base lies toward the center, the cutting moves from the diagonal fold toward the V/H fold. It is important to realize that in all RO motifs, the cutting is counterclockwise and the motif's V, point, or base lies toward the center of the overlay.

For a left-orientation heart, the marking is done along the right-hand fold. In this orientation, the point of the heart lies *away* from the center of the overlay. To cut, rotate the prebasted overlay so that the center of the overlay lies on the left and the outer edges of the overlay lie on the right. The cutting of the spiral will be counterclockwise in direction.

Left-handed people, beware! For you, the RO heart will be marked on the right and the LO heart on the left. Cutting will remain clockwise as usual.

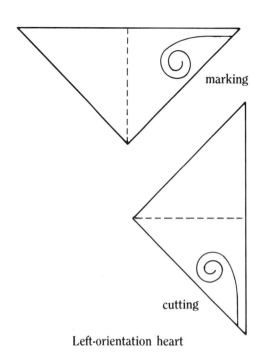

marking

cutting

Left-orientation heart

Basic Hearts*

Fold	Snailhouses.
Two-step marking	Both sides are identical with RO hearts.* For RO hearts, the point begins ⅜" from the center of the overlay; the center of the spiral lies on a line 2¾" from the center of the overlay; the center of the circle lies 1⅛" from the left diagonal fold; the circle is 1½" in diameter.
Precutting	Cut the heart completely. Make a tiny snip for the corner arrows (see Corners).
Finish	Simple (see Finishes).
Embellishment	Dog's Foot (see Embellishments).

*The basic rules of orientation do not apply for hearts. See Basic Heart instructions.

Basic Heart Motif

Unit III Combinations, Secondary Motifs, and Variations

1 Categories of Pa nDau Appliqué Designs

The star, snailhouse, elephant's foot, ram's head, and heart are all distinct in both appearance and technique. These are *primary motifs*. They are easily recognized. They set the basic tone of the overall design. And, when combined with other motifs, they usually maintain their basic structure and distinctive properties. If two or more such primary motifs are used together, the overall design is a *combination*. Combination designs can be deceptive. For example, one may use RO snailhouses with LO rams' heads, with simple two-step marking that is identical for both sides of the prebasted overlay. Usually, however, in a combination design, the primary motifs remain separate and readily recognizable.

A *complex* design is one that requires more than one fold for the precutting, two-part basting, and/or extreme postcutting. *Elephant's Foot* is a primary motif, but a complex design if the rings are precut along the V/H fold. The Color Section includes a fascinating blue-on-blue design that, due to its interlocking motifs, might be included in the complex category. For such a design, there may be a number of approaches to folding and precutting.

There are many minor, less distinct motifs that balance the overall design or simply fill in empty spaces between the primary motifs. These are *secondary motifs* and, in general, they complement the primary motif in the piece. They vary greatly in technique, shape, intricacy, and visual effect and, used creatively, can elevate a design from routine to fascinating. A design that has a primary motif and secondary motifs is called a *variation*.

The most common of the secondary motifs are rings, plumes, bars, and center and corner treatments. In general, these secondary motifs are only partially cut into the prebasted overlay, and in nearly all cases, the primary motifs are stitched completely before any stitching on the secondary motifs is begun. This is a minor contradiction of the standard rules of quilting and needlework, which recommend beginning at the center of a piece and working outward. In pa ndau appliqué, you may work

back and forth, from the center to the edge, and back toward the center again. The best rule is to stitch those motifs that can cause major shifting of the layers first and the less risky motifs last. According to this rule, snailhouses will always be stitched first and corner arrows last.

The identification and classification of pa ndau appliqué designs are fascinating exercises in geometric analysis. Because secondary designs usually do not interfere with the visual impact of the primary motif, all variations will be identified according to the primary motif.

Only in rare instances does the addition of secondary motifs result in a variation with a specific name. Two obvious and important examples are *Spiderweb* and *Elephant's Foot*. *Spiderweb* is the name some Hmong apply to a basic star with multiple corner arrows, with an arbitrary number of channels in the star itself. (Some Hmong reject the use of the name for the star variation, reserving it for a difficult mazelike design.)

A more universal exception is *Elephant's Foot*, which is nothing more than a simple circle of four snailhouse pairs surrounded by two or more rings. Rings are a common secondary motif, and yet this overall design is so popular and so recognizable that the variation has earned its own name and joins the ranks as a primary motif with its own series of variations.

The final category of pa ndau appliqué is *allover designs*. They are relatively few in number, and they are distinct and graphic. One, the Saw-toothed Squares design, uses a popular center motif (secondary) in repeats that are set square or diagonally across the entire piece. This illustrates the potential of any secondary motif to become a primary motif. In general, allover designs rely upon full mastery of postcutting and the keen eye and patience that come with experience. Because of the skill level they require, the examples of allover design are shown in a special chapter on foundation cutting (See Unit III, Chapter 4.)

The five categories of pa ndau appliqué are general. There are many designs that could be placed in more than one category; others seem to merit a class of their own. But the five categories explained here are adequate guidelines in analyzing pa ndau designs.

Categories of Pa ndau Appliqué Designs

1 Simple — one primary motif (RO and/or LO).

2 Variation — one primary motif with any number of secondary motifs.

3 Combination — two or more primary motifs with the possible addition of secondary motifs.

4 Complex — a design that requires more than one fold and/or two-part basting.

5 Allover — a motif (primary or secondary) that is repeated across the design.

2 Secondary Motifs

Rings

Rings are the most common of the secondary motifs. They are most often used with a circle of snailhouses, forming the popular *Elephant's Foot* design. But they offer many other design possibilities as well.

Rings may be used in pairs or triplets surrounding a snailhouse, or on the inside of a circle of snailhouses. For a lacy effect, encase the snailhouses in one inner and one outer ring.

Multiple rings can create a lovely echo effect. However, the farther the outermost ring is from the primary motif, the less it will resemble that motif. This is a pitfall common to multiple rings, because the scale and change in character of the outer rings can easily overwhelm the smaller, central primary motif.

Rings can also surround hearts, rams' heads, and isolated snailhouse pairs. A ring may adopt the saw-toothed edge of the dragon's tail or take on the shape of any secondary motif that it happens to encase.

Plumes

A plume motif is usually an extension of a simple ring; only rarely will a design include a plume that "floats" separate of a ring. The three parts of a plume are the *tip*, the *side*, and the *base*, which is the bottom of the

plume or the point at which it joins a ring. Because the tips and sides of the plumes may be cut in a wide range of angles, many visual effects can be achieved. See Design Exercise 1 in Chapter 5 of this unit for an especially lacy design with simple and floating plumes.

The specifications for precutting a plume are detailed and must be precise. The measurements for the tip indicate both the distance the tip lies from the center of the

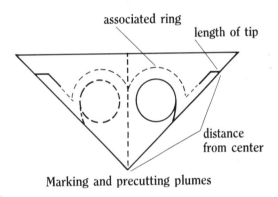

Marking and precutting plumes

folded overlay and the length of the tip (from the point to the beginning of the side). The incline of the tip depends on the angle at which the incision is made and is left to your discretion. The second specification for a plume gives the distance from the center of the overlay to the base of the plume. *In most cases, this specification is identical to that marking the associated ring and is not provided separately in the directions for a design.* The length of the side of the plume depends upon the angle of the tip and, therefore, cannot be listed in the directions.

To precut a plume, cut the entire tip and only ¼″ of the side. If the plume is to be combined with a ring, precut the ring only on the folds that do not have plumes.

An exception to the usual precutting method is the open plume. In addition to the specifications for the plume and ring, a notation for a base ring will be made.

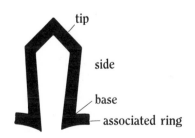

Parts of a plume

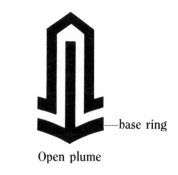

Open plume

Floating plume

Squared rings

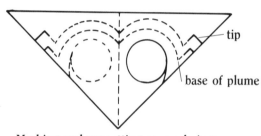

Marking and precutting squared rings

Precut the plume as usual, cutting the associated ring on non-plume folds. Then precut the base ring on all folds. Completely postcut and stitch the plumes and ring before stitching the base ring. Postcut along the midline of the plume to "open" it, beginning at the base ring and ending a channel's width from the stitched top of the plume. Stitch the opening, then stitch the base ring in segments according to the usual procedure.

Echoing plumes are an effective solution to the problem of empty corners in a design (see EF-3). Plumes are also used in quadrant designs, and they may join with rings in encasing virtually any primary motif.

Squared Rings

An ingenious combination of the plume and ring motifs produces a squared ring. The precutting for this variation is two-part. Along the V/H fold, cut as for a simple ring. Along the diagonal fold, cut as you would for a plume with a flat tip. Practice this on paper until you learn to judge the proper size of the side of the plume, so that the base of the plume lies in line with the V of the ring. As the rings echo farther from the center, the flat portion of the plume becomes larger until any resemblance to a plume is lost.

Bars

Bars divide the overall design into four quadrants. They may lie along the vertical and horizontal folds, creating a cross, or they may lie along both diagonals, forming an X. *Complete bars* meet at the center of the overlay. *Partial bars,* as the name implies, do not meet. Bars range from simple, straight channels to ornate geometric designs, but they never extend to the finished edge of the design. Visually, bars help the viewer analyze the quadrant symmetry of a design.

Whether bars are to be complete or partial, do not cut more than ¼" into the prebasted overlay. More extensive cutting will increase the risk of distorting the design.

Vertical/horizontal bars. If vertical/horizontal bars are complete, they may be partially cut into the prebasted overlay. For the square fold, simply slide one scissor

Vertical/horizontal bars

Diagonal bars

Partial bars

Partial diagonal bars

blade inside the horizontal fold at the center and cut; this cut will produce only the horizontal bar. To produce the vertical bars, slide the scissor points into the openings created by the horizontal cut and make snips along the two vertical folds. For V/H bars from a snailhouse fold, make a temporary crease along the V/H fold *after* prebasting; one cut along this line is all that is required. Do not cut the outer edge. For the star fold, vertical/horizontal bars must be postcut.

For partial bars, all cutting must be done after the primary motifs have been stitched. Use a ruler to measure the beginning and end of each bar so that they will be uniform (see SH-7).

Diagonal bars. Complete diagonal bars are easily precut into a snailhouse fold. Three separate cuts are needed to accomplish the four snips. The first is along the right-hand fold, making two of the four bars. Make the other two bars by cutting along the left-hand folds (two separate cuts). If the star fold is made according to the instructions, it will be possible to produce the bars with one cut by sliding one blade of the scissors inside the diagonal foldline. Complete bars may be precut into the pinwheel fold, but must be postcut in both envelope folds.

For all folds, partial bars should be postcut along the diagonal foldlines after the primary motifs have been stitched.

Complex bars. The ends of bars may be flat-ended, square, or circular, depending on the overall design. Because bars are always cut after all other motifs are stitched, you can decide what effect you want to complement the rest of the design. Elaborate bars can sometimes become the primary motif, as in Snailhouse-9. Bars may also be used in conjunction with a center motif, as in Heart-7.

Complex bars with circular ends

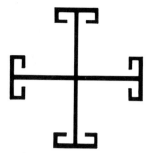

Complex bars with square ends

Fences

In many designs, a diamond-in-a-square effect is created by including a reverse appliquéd "fence." (This

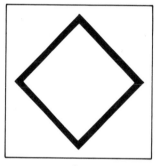

Simple fence

term is strictly American.) Fences range from a simple channel to a zigzag dragon's tail, and the sides may meet at the corners or they may overlap.

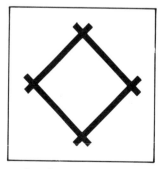

Overlapping extensions

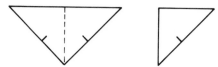

Markings for fences lie perpendicular to the diagonal folds.

For star and snailhouse folds, make a ¼ " snip in the diagonal folds, *holding the scissors perpendicular to the diagonal fold.* For square folds, two snips will be required — one on the vertical and one on the horizontal fold. Mark the distance from the center on both folds and cut along the imaginary line which connects the two markings. For all folds, the marking and precutting for complete fences should lie slightly closer to the center of the overlay than the midpoint of the diagonal fold. This provides allowance for the hem along the outside edge. For designs based on envelope or pinwheel folds, fences should be postcut. A simple but effective fence may be seen in Ram's Head-1.

For overlapping corners, the initial snips should lie closer to the center of the folded overlay so that there is ample space between the fence corner and the outer edge for the extensions of the fence rails.

Partial fences, such as the one in Ram's Head-3, cannot be precut because the channels do not extend to any of the lines of symmetry. If you like, mark them with a water-erasable marker before postcutting.

For an example of a zigzag, or picket fence, see the daisy wheel design in Design Exercise 2. To duplicate this, cut one side of the fence and stitch the flat side of the channel. Then cut the zigzag according to the instructions for the dragon's tail explained later in this chapter.

For variations, you may try double channels (mark and cut two snips), starlike eight-sided fences, or even a double-sided zigzag. In extreme cases, the fence may become the primary motif, and it may be incorporated into other motifs of the design (Design Exercise 6).

Corners

Corner treatments serve two purposes. They can be part of the original plan, or they can be last-minute remedies for an imbalance of color or a poorly balanced design. For simplicity, this discussion will include any secondary corner motifs that lie on the V/H axes or anywhere along the diagonal axes, as well as those in the corner of the square overlay. For best results, test your cutting on paper first.

Arrows are the most common corner motifs and, with the addition of rickrack cutting, they can be quite elaborate. Chicken feet is a whimsical corner motif, sometimes combined with a partial fence. The chevron, a heavy treatment for a corner, adds sophistication to the simplest of designs (see S-4).

The clam and worm motifs (both Hmong names) require considerable space along the diagonal lines of symmetry and add an angular touch to the overall design. An enlarged clam can have a bladelike appearance resembling complex diagonal bars. The clam motif is a cross-section view from the side — an image different from the clamshell pattern known to American quilters.

If your design lacks interest at the middle of the sides (V/H axes), pairs of corner arrows may be used to enhance the primary motifs. When these arrows appear along the V/H axes *and* in the corners, the design is obviously divided into quadrants. These "quadrant corners" create a strong secondary motif. Because quadrant corners lie inside the vertical and horizontal axes, they must be postcut. The diagrams suggest other motifs that would enhance the N-S-E-W positions on a square (SH-3). Creative use of corner motifs can make the difference between a simply routine pa ndau piece and a striking example of geometric design. Examine the pa ndau in the Color Section and pay particular attention to the balance and completeness corner motifs can supply.

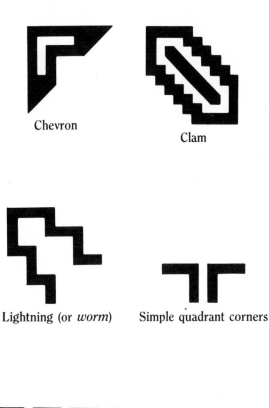

Chevron

Clam

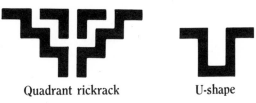

Lightning (or *worm*)

Simple quadrant corners

Quadrant rickrack

U-shape

Arrow #1   Arrow #2   Arrow #3

Rickrack   Chicken feet

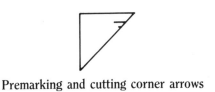

Complex design

Premarking and cutting corner arrows

41

To mark arrows, you need only know the distance from the center to the incision. For chevrons and rickrack, a pair of incisions must be cut. The cutting for all corner arrows must be parallel to the outer edge of the folded overlay. For the clam, chicken feet, and motifs along the V/H axes, postcutting is recommended. With a little practice, you will soon be able to analyze these motifs and devise methods and measurements for precutting.

Centers

The greatest variation in complexity and technique lies in this category of secondary motifs. Each type of center must be considered separately. Because the fold required for a center often is not the same used for the rest of the design, the center may have to be postcut. For the seldom-used envelope and pinwheel folds, no specific instructions are included for the center. In these cases, experiment with paper cutting to find the best way to cut the center design.

Bull's-eye (square, snailhouse, and star folds). This motif is the best example of radial symmetry in pa ndau appliqué. Determine the distance from the center of the folded overlay to the first ring, and the distance between the rings. Then mark these points on the V/H and diagonal folds. Because the actual cuts must be circular, make only a tiny snip on the folded overlay. Cut no more than one ring at a time.

Bull's-eye

Sunshine (square, snailhouse, and star folds). This central motif is a variation of the bull's-eye. The distance between the next-to-last and last rings must be greater than the others to allow for the depth of the zigzag cutting. For cutting tips, refer to the section on dragon's tail.

Sunshine

Simple Cross or X (square, snailhouse, and star folds). This quietly effective central motif is excellent for beginners. For the square fold, slit the overlay along the V/H folds for the inner cross and, for the outer channel, make tiny snips perpendicular to the vertical and

Simple cross

horizontal folds. For the snailhouse fold, temporarily fold the prebasted overlay along the vertical axis and snip the top of the cross perpendicular to the axis. Restore the overlay to the snailhouse fold and cut along the vertical fold for the inner cross. After the inner cross

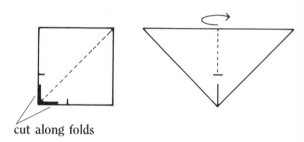

cut along folds

Precutting for simple cross

has been stitched, postcut the outer channel in small segments. This channel can be precut into snailhouse and star folds, but use caution to cut *only* the V/H folds, and always perpendicular to the fold. For the star fold, only the outer channel can be precut.

The same procedure is used to cut an X motif, or a cross that lies on the diagonal. Simply cut along the diagonal folds, snipping the outer channel perpendicular to the diagonal fold.

The inner cross or X is actually the background in this motif, and it matches the design. You may add any number of outer channels to the cross or X by making a series of equidistant snips in the precutting stage. The more outer channels you add, the less dominant the inner cross will be.

Reverse Cross (square, star, and snailhouse folds). The reverse cross has the same geometric effect on a design as the regular cross, but it alters the color balance of the piece. The inner cross, which is actually the overlay, gains its shape from the channel around it. No cuts are made along the V/H folds for this motif. Only the snips

Reverse cross

perpendicular to the V/H folds are precut. For the star fold, only one cut is necessary. For the square fold, make two cuts — one on the vertical axis and one on the horizontal axis. For the snailhouse fold, temporarily fold the overlay along the V/H axes and make one cut. Again, be careful not to accidentally cut a diagonal fold.

A reverse X can be precut with snips perpendicular to the diagonal axes.

Compass and Reverse Compass (square, star, and snailhouse folds). These two central motifs are basically the same as the cross and reverse cross. The difference is that the snips that are precut for the outer channel

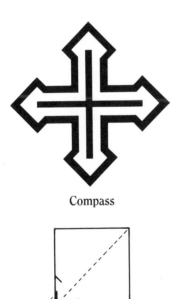

Compass

cut along folds

Precutting the compass motif

are not made perpendicular to the fold into which they are cut. Instead, the snips made in the V/H folds are made perpendicular to the *diagonal axes* for each of the three common folds.

The compass points can be made straight or with barbs, as shown in the diagram. The barbs are postcut.

Steps (star fold). Steps 1 and 2 (see diagrams) require cutting in the V/H folds *and* the diagonal folds. If your design is based on the square or snailhouse fold, make a temporary extra fold *after* prebasting so that the overlay is actually star-folded. Add a bit of basting in the center to secure. Cut, remove this secondary basting, then precut the remainder of the design.

Steps 1

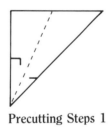

Precutting Steps 1

The center of Steps 1 can contain another smaller motif, such as circles or a cross. It is also an ideal motif for appliquéd embellishment.

Steps 2

Star and Steps (star variation): This design illustrates
the lovely effect of using multiple secondary motifs.
Author's collection.

For Steps 3, the precutting is the same as that for
Steps 2, but the postcutting differs. *Do not cut* the ends
of the cross in either the inner or outer channels. As

shown in the diagram, leaving the ends uncut creates
a windowpane effect. Embroidered triangles further
enhance the stairstep effect. An exquisite example of
this center motif can be seen in Star-9.

The Hmong call all of these center steps *worms* due
to the basic zigzag nature of the motifs.

Stars and Cobweb (star fold). Make precut snips on
both the V/H and diagonal folds, perpendicular to the
opposite fold, as you would for a basic star. As you
postcut the sides of the web, make gentle swags from

Marking Steps 2 and 3

Steps 3

Cobweb

44

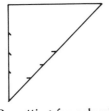

Precutting for cobweb

Fletch (arrow feathers)

point to point. The web may be comprised of two or more rings. You may want to add a tiny appliqué or reverse-appliquéd circle in the center.

Daisy Wheel (star fold). This motif has a softness that can be effective in pa ndau. It combines the cutting techniques for the basic star with the rings of the elephant's foot. The innermost snips mark the bottom of the airspace between the petals, which will not be connected to one another. Cut out each of these bits of fabric as you stitch around the daisy, curving the outer petals. Complete the ring in the usual manner.

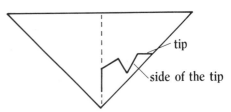

Marking and precutting for *fletch*

fold. The base of the subunit lies along the V/H fold, but cannot be precut due to the center shaft of the arrow. The tip is precut parallel to the outer edge of the overlay, and the side of the tip may also be precut. The diagram indicates the postcut third, fourth, and fifth sides as dotted lines.

Daisy wheel

Dragon's tail

The term dragon's tail can be used generically to describe any saw-toothed edge in pa ndau appliqué, or applied specifically to a variation of snailhouse in which one side of the spiral is cut into an ever-tightening ridge of triangles. This serrated edge is always produced by postcutting.

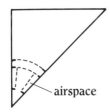

Marking and precutting for daisy wheel

Fletch, or Arrow Feathers (star, snailhouse fold). This motif is symbolic of feathers on an arrow, an instrument important to the Hmong for their survival. The motif represents the view of the arrow down the shaft from the blunt end.

The motif, which has four identical subunits, can be marked and precut using either the star or snailhouse

Dragon's tail motif

45

Hearts and Rings (variation with dragon's tail motif):
The dragon's tail edge is meticulously outlined with
gold thread to create an exquisite pa ndau design.
Author's collection.

If the primary motif is a snailhouse pair, it must be a simplified version. It should either be enlarged or limited to a few rings, so that ample fabric is available between the rings for the toothed cutting. As the diagram illustrates, the original precutting of the snailhouse spiral is "off-center" in the completed motif. The concave edge, which is left plain and simple, should be stitched almost to the core. Use a ⅛″ seam allowance so that a wide strip will remain for the notched cutting. Then cut and stitch a few triangles at a time along the convex curve, beginning at the V. At the core of the spiral, the triangles should extend slightly around the tip to the concave side, like a saucy flip of the tail. A dragon's tail is a seemingly endless challenge of points to be turned and V's to be clipped! The needle artist who is as gifted with design as she is with her needle will be able to create a realistic tail if she cuts the rings of the snailhouse so that they become narrower toward the core. Tipping the notches in the direction of the

tightening spiral will also enhance the playful character of the dragon's tail.

The spiraling dragon's tail is used on other primary and secondary motifs that have a curve or spiral. The heart, ram's head, and rings of the elephant's foot are often chosen for this treatment. In all of these examples,

Playful dragon's tail motif

the motifs are simplified and are spaced farther apart than usual to accommodate notching. It is common to see these serrated variations couched in gold thread. These are the deluxe examples of a needle artist's mastery of pa ndau appliqué.

Several stunning pieces and one whimsical example of dragon's tail are shown in the Color Section.

Designs consisting of secondary motifs only

In many pa ndau appliqué designs, several motifs are combined so effectively that one scarcely notices the absence of a primary motif. These are combinations, because no one motif is dominant. Combining center motifs with fences and corner treatments can be a wonderful means to explore geometric paper cutting, because it is so easy to plan as you go. To spur your imagination and challenge your creativity, analyze the examples shown here, duplicate them, or create your own!

Secondary Motif 1 is based on a star fold. The clam motifs in the corners, as well as snips for the W's and center circle, can all be precut. The design is only intermediate in difficulty, yet it provides great diversity of technique, with both zigzags and perfect circles.

Secondary Motif 2 is based upon the square and star fold, and it requires complex marking. This is because the snailhouse motifs, which are in right orientation but lie on the V/H axes, must be cut on the folds of the

square, while the clam and "blades" must be cut on the diagonal folds. To precut the design, fold and baste for the square fold. Mark RO snailhouses. Then fold along the diagonal to complete the star fold. Precut the clams and central circle.

Secondary Motif 3 has snailhouse motifs that can be precut into a square-folded overlay according to the instructions for Secondary Motif 2. At most, a tiny snip or two can be precut to indicate the central motif. For the remaining circles, use a circle stencil for accurate marking and foundation cutting.

Secondary Motif 2: Clams and Bull's-eye

Secondary Motif 1: Clams and Sunshine

Secondary Motif 3: Sunshine and Circles

3 Variations

The following specifications will help you create a wide range of designs — all variations on the techniques and designs you have studied. *Note:* When you stack the layers for foundation basting, place the marked side of the overlay *down*. Failure to do so for asymmetrical designs will result in designs that are mirror images of the photograph.

S-1: Basic Star with Arrows

S-1	Basic Star with Arrows (often called *Spiderweb).*	**Precutting**	Cut a ³⁄₁₆″ snip at all eight markings.
Fold	Star.	**Postcutting**	After foundation basting, cut the three channels for the star one or two segments at a time. Add the arrows at the four corners.
Marking	V/H fold: 2″, 2½″, 3″ from the center of the overlay.		
	Eight-point fold: 2″, 2½″, 3″, 3½″, 4″ from the center of the overlay.	**Finish**	Double channel (see Finishes).
		Embellishment	Center diamonds (see Embellishments).

S-2: Twinkling Star

S-2	Twinkling Star.	
Fold	Star.	
Precut	*V/H fold:* 1½″, 1¹⁵⁄₁₆″, 2⅜″, 2¹³⁄₁₆″, 3¼″, and 3¹¹⁄₁₆″ from the center of the overlay.	

S-2 Twinkling Star.

Fold Star.

Precut *V/H fold:* $1\frac{1}{2}''$, $1\frac{15}{16}''$, $2\frac{3}{8}''$, $2\frac{13}{16}''$, $3\frac{1}{4}''$, and $3\frac{11}{16}''$ from the center of the overlay.

Eight-point fold: Same as V/H fold.

Precutting Cut a $\frac{3}{16}''$ snip at all twelve markings.

Postcutting After foundation basting, cut only the five innermost channels for the star in segments. The outermost series of snips *do not* form a channel. Instead, they are cut and stitched as eight-corner arrows.

Finish Simple (see Finishes).

Embellishment Diamonds (see Embellishments).

S-3: Basic Star with Flying V's

S-3	Basic Star with Flying V's.		overlay.
Fold	Star.	**Precutting**	Cut a 3/16″ snip at all eight markings.
Marking	*V/H fold*: 1½″, 2″, and 2½″ from the	**Postcutting**	After foundation basting, cut the three
	center of the overlay.		channels for the star in segments.
	Eight-point fold: 1½″, 2″, 2½″, 3″	**Finish**	Inverted sawtooth (see Finishes).
	and 3½″ from the center of the	**Embellishment**	Center diamonds (see Embellishments).

S-4
SH
EF
RH
H

S-4: Basic Star with Corner Chevrons

S-4	Basic Star with Corner Chevrons.	
Fold	Star.	
Marking	*V/H fold:* 1½″, 2″, 2½″, 3″, and 3½″ from the center of the overlay.	

Eight-point fold: 1½″, 2″, 2½″, 3″, 3½″, 4″, 4½″, and 5″ from the center of the overlay.

Precutting Cut a ³⁄₁₆″ snip at all thirteen markings.

Postcutting After foundation basting, cut the five channels for the star in segments. Three precuts still remain. The outermost and innermost of the three join to form the outline of the chevron. Cut and stitch. The inner bar or channel is last to be completed.

Finish Simple (see Finishes).

Embellishment Center diamonds (see Embellishments).

51

SH-1: Basic Snailhouses (right orientation)

SH-1
Fold
Two-step
marking

Basic Snailhouses (right orientation).*
Snailhouse.
Both sides are identical with RO snailhouses. The incision lies 2¼″ from the center of the overlay. The center of the circle lies 1″ from the right fold. The circle is 1¼″ in diameter.

Precutting Completely cut the snailhouses.
Detail No more than three rings are advised for beginners.
Finish Sawtooth (see Finishes).
Embellishment Diamonds in circles (see Embellishments).

*Full understanding of the terms right and left orientation is essential. The terms apply to both the appearance *and* marking and cutting techniques of snailhouses.

SH-2: Basic Snailhouses (left orientation)

SH-2 **Fold** **Two-step** **marking**	Basic Snailhouses (left orientation).* Snailhouse. Both sides are identical with LO snailhouses. The incision lies 2¼″ from the center of the overlay. The center of the circle lies 1″ from the left fold. The circle is 1¼″ in diameter.	**Precutting** **Detail** **Finish** **Embellishment**	Completely cut the snailhouses. Cut three or four rings in the snailhouses. Single channel (see Finishes). Water Lilies (see Embellishments).

*Full understanding of the terms right and left orientation is essential. The terms apply to both the appearance *and* marking and cutting techniques of snailhouses.

SH-3: Diagonal Snailhouses (right and left orientation)

SH-3	Diagonal Snailhouses (right and left orientation).
Fold	Snailhouse.
Two-step marking	The two sides of the overlay are different.

First side: For RO snailhouses, the incision lies ⅞" from the center of the overlay. The center of the circle lies ⅞" from the right fold. The circle is 1¼" in diameter. For LO snailhouses, the incision lies 3¼" from the center of the overlay. The center of the circle lies ⅞" from the left fold. The circle is 1¼" in diameter.

Second side: For LO snailhouses only, same as LO for first side.

Both sides (optional): You may mark the inner pair of arrows (1¾" and 2¾" from the center of the overlay) and the corner arrows (5" from the center of the overlay).

Precutting	Completely cut the snailhouses. Practice cutting the arrows on paper so that you can check the angles (see Corners).
Postcutting	Cut the remaining arrows.
Finish	Simple (See Finishes).

SH-4: Pinwheel Snailhouses

SH-4	Pinwheel Snailhouses.	
Fold	Envelope.	
Four-step marking	All four sections are identical. Orient the folded overlay so that the folds lie right-left and top-bottom. Mark a RO snailhouse. The incision lies 3″ from the top or bottom of the sides. The center of the circle lies 1″ from the fold. The circle is 1¾″ in diameter. Rotate the overlay and repeat for the	

marking of the remaining three sides.

Cutting Completely cut the snailhouses.

Detail Because the circle is so large, you may cut as many as five rings.

Postcutting Make a template for a heart 1″ high and 1¼″ at widest point. Mark and cut eight hearts according to the photograph.

Finish Simple (see Finishes).

Embellishment Diamonds (see Embellishments).

SH-5: Snailhouses with Plumes

SH-5	Snailhouses with Plumes.	Precutting	Completely cut the snailhouses. Cut
Fold	Snailhouse.		the top and side of the plume, ending
Two-step	Both sides are identical with RO		½″ from the rim of the snailhouse. Cut
marking	snailhouses. The incision lies 2½″		a snip for the corner arrows.

SH-5
Fold
Two-step
marking

Snailhouses with Plumes.
Snailhouse.
Both sides are identical with RO snailhouses. The incision lies 2½″ from the center of the overlay. The center of the circle lies ⅞″ from the folds. The circle is 1½″ in diameter. *Plume:* 4½″ from the center of the overlay; the tip is ½″ in length. *Corner arrow:* 5″ from the center of the overlay.

Precutting   Completely cut the snailhouses. Cut the top and side of the plume, ending ½″ from the rim of the snailhouse. Cut a snip for the corner arrows.

Postcutting   Cut and stitch the ring around the snailhouses one segment at a time. The ring should lie ½″ outside the snailhouses.

Finish   Simple (see Finishes).

Embellishment   Center diamonds (see Embellishments).

SH-6: Quadrant Snailhouses with Plumes

SH-6
Fold
Two-step marking

Quadrant Snailhouses (with plumes). Snailhouse.

Both sides are identically marked, each with one RO and one LO snailhouse, plus double plumes. For RO snailhouses the incision lies 3⅛″ from the center of the overlay. The center of the circle lies ⅝″ from the fold. The circle is ⅞″ in diameter. For LO snailhouses the incision lies 1⅞″ from the center of the overlay. The center of the circle lies ⅝″ from the fold. The circle is ⅞″ in diameter.

Outer plume: Tip lies 4¾″ from center of the overlay. The length of the tip is ⅜″.

Precutting

Completely cut the snailhouses. Cut a ⅜″ snip for the tip of the plume. Cut the sides of the plume, ending ⅜″ from the rim of the snailhouse.

Detail

It will be possible to cut only two rings in the snailhouse.

Postcutting

Using a washable marker, draw the two diagonals of the overlay. Mark tips of the inner plumes ⅜″ from the center of the overlay along each diagonal. Cut. The ring is postcut ⅜″ outside the rims of the snailhouses. The other two plumes in each quadrant are also postcut.

Finish

Simple (see Finishes).

SH-7: Pinwheel Snailhouses with Double Plumes

SH-7	Pinwheel Snailhouses (with double plumes).	**Precutting**	Completely cut the snailhouses. Cut the top and sides of both plumes, ending ⅜″ from the rim of the snailhouses.
Fold	Envelope.		
Four-step marking	All four sections of the overlay are marked in the same manner. Rotate the prebasted overlay so that the folds lie top-bottom and right-left. For RO snailhouses, the incision is 3″ from the top or bottom of the fold. The center of the circle lies ¾″ from the fold. The circle is 1⅜″ in diameter.	**Postcutting**	With a washable marker, mark the remaining two plumes in each quadrant, marking tips at ¼″ and 5¼″ from the center on the diagonals. Cut. Also cut the ring ⅜″ from the rims of the snailhouses. Cut bars along the vertical and horizontal axes.
	Plumes: Tips lie 2″ above and below the incision. The length of the tips is ⅜″.	**Finish**	Simple (see Finishes).

58

SH-8: Flying Snailhouses

SH-8
Fold
Three-step
marking

Flying Snailhouses.
Snailhouse.
The three steps are all different for this unusual design. The center two snailhouses lie on the vertical line of symmetry.
For the first side: Mark a LO snailhouse. The incision lies 3⅜″ from the center of the overlay. The center of the circle lies 1″ from the fold. The circle is 1¼″ in diameter.
For the second side: Mark a LO snailhouse according to the first side. Fold the overlay along the vertical axis and crease. Mark a LO snailhouse on the vertical axis. The incision lies 1″ from the center of the overlay on the left diagonal foldline. The center of the circle lies 1″ from the center of the overlay. The circle is 1¼″ in diameter.
For the third side: Turn the overlay to the first side. Mark a "flying" RO snailhouse on the vertical axis. The incision is at the junction of the vertical fold and the rim of the central snailhouse. The center of the circle lies 3″ from the center of the overlay on the V/H axes. The circle is 1¼″ in diameter.

Precutting Completely cut the central snailhouse and then the "flying" snailhouse. (It will be cut in right orientation.) Finally, cut the two LO snailhouses.
Finish Simple (see Finishes).
Embellishment Pinwheels (see Embellishments).

SH-9: Fireworks

SH-9	Fireworks.	*Second side:* Central RO snailhouse.
Fold	Envelope — two-step method.	The incision lies 3″ along the diagonal
	Note: For this unusual fold, the center	of the overlay. The center of the cir-
	of the overlay *is not* the point of a V	cle lies ⅝″ from the diagonal fold. The
	made by the right and left diagonals.	circle is ⅞″ in diameter. Mark a cen-
Two-step	*First side:* Two RO snailhouses. The	tral LO snailhouse along the left fold
marking	incisions lie 1¾″ and 4¼″ along the	with specifications identical to the cen-
	right diagonal of the overlay. Both	tral RO snailhouse.
	circles lie ⅝″ from the diagonal fold.	*Note:* The rims of the two central
	Both circles are ⅞″ in diameter. These	snailhouses should lie exactly between
	are the inner and outer snailhouses.	the inner and outer snailhouses. Re-
	Mark two LO snailhouses along the left	mark them if necessary. (The flying
	diagonal with specifications identical to	snailhouses may be postcut.)
	the inner and outer RO snailhouses.	
	The "flying" snailhouses are drawn in	**Precutting** Completely cut all snailhouses.
	relationship to the V/H axes. The in-	**Postcutting** Cut the bar design after the outer edge
	cision lies 1″ from the center of the	has been finished.
	overlay. The center of the circle lies	**Finish** Simple (see Finishes). It is recom-
	¾″ from the V/H fold. The circle is	mended that the outer edge of the
	⅞″ in diameter.	overlay be stitched before the complex
		bar design is cut.

EF-1: Inverted Elephant's Foot (left orientation)

EF-1	Inverted Elephant's Foot (LO).	
Fold	Snailhouse/Star.	
Complex marking	Temporarily fold along the V/H axes, basting if necessary (see Basic Elephant's Foot). On the V/H folds, mark rings 2⅝″, 3″, and 3⅜″ from the center of the overlay; snip. Restore to snailhouse fold and proceed with marking. Both sides are identical with LO snailhouses. The incision lies 2″ from the center of the overlay. The center of the circle lies ⅞″ from the lefthand fold. The circle is 1¼″ in diameter.	

Rings: 2⅝″, 3″, and 3⅜″ from the center of the overlay (see Basic Elephant's Foot).

Precutting Completely cut the snailhouses. Cut no more than 1/16″ to ⅛″ snips along the folds to indicate the rings.

Postcutting After the snailhouses have been stitched, cut and stitch the rings one segment at a time. The rings should lie ⅜″ from the rims of the snailhouses.

Finish Simple (see Finishes).

Embellishment Pinwheel (see Embellishments).

EF-2: Inverted Elephant's Foot with Inner and Outer Rings

EF-2	Inverted Elephant's Foot (LO) with Inner and Outer Rings.*
Fold	Snailhouse/Star.
Complex marking	Temporarily fold along the V/H axes, basting if necessary (see Basic Elephant's Foot). On the V/H folds, mark rings 2″ and 2½″ from the center of the overlay and snip. Restore to snailhouse fold and proceed with marking. Both sides are identical with LO snailhouses. The incision lies 2½″ from the center of the overlay. The center of the circle lies 1″ from the left-hand fold. The circle is 1⅜″ in diameter. *Rings:* 2″ and 3″ from the center of the overlay (see Basic Elephant's Foot).
Precutting	Completely cut the snailhouses. Cut no more than 1/16″ to 1/8″ snips along the folds to indicate the rings.
Postcutting	After the snailhouses have been stitched, cut and stitch the rings one segment at a time. The rings should lie 3/16″ outside both sides of the snailhouses.
Finish	Simple (see Finishes).
Embellishment	Center and corner diamonds (see Embellishments).

*The outer rings curve very deeply into the V/H axes to enhance the lacy effect. This causes a difference in the specifications for the marking along the V/H and diagonal axes.

EF-3: Elephant's Foot with Plumes

EF-3	Elephant's Foot with Plumes.
Fold	Snailhouse/Star. (Optional addition of center cross requires star fold — see Center Motifs).
Complex marking	Temporarily fold along the V/H axes, basting if necessary (see Basic Elephant's Foot). On the V/H fold, mark rings 2¾″, 3⅛″, and 3½″ from the center of the overlay and snip. Restore to snailhouse fold and proceed with marking. Both sides are identical with RO snailhouses. The incision lies 2¼″ from the center of the overlay. The center of the circle lies 1″ from the right-hand fold. The circle is 1⅜″ in diameter. *Base ring:* 2¾″ from the center of the overlay. *Plumes:* 4¾″ and 5⅛″ from the center of the overlays. Length of inner tip is ½″.
Precutting	Completely cut the snailhouses. For the plume at the 4¾″ mark, snip a ½″ tip. Then cut no more than 1″ along the side of the plume. For the plume

at the 5⅛″ mark, cut only a ⅛″ snip into the fold, parallel to the tip of the inner plume. Cut a snip for the base ring in the diagonal folds.

Postcutting	Extensive foundation basting is required. *Step 1:* After the snailhouses have been stitched, stitch the plumes that have tips 4¾″ from the center and the associated rings, which should be cut ⅝″ from the snailhouses. *Step 2:* Cut the center out of each plume and cut the base ring between the ring from Step 1 and the snailhouses. This ring lies 5⁄16″ from the snailhouses. *Step 3:* Beginning at the snip for the 5⅛″ mark on one of the diagonal folds, cut another set of plumes and rings 5⁄16″ outside the plumes and rings from Step 1.
Finish	Simple (see Finishes).
Embellishment	The reverse-appliqué center cross may be postcut or may be marked and partially precut (see Center Motifs).

EF-4: Simplified Elephant's Foot

EF-4	Simplified Elephant's Foot.	lie on the V/H fold.
Fold	Snailhouse/Star.	*Rings:* Mark rings 1½", 2", and 2½" from the center on *both* the right and left folds.
Complex marking	Temporarily fold along the V/H axes, basting if necessary (see Basic Elephant's Foot). On the V/H fold, mark rings 2¼", 2⅝", and 3" from the center of the overlay and snip. Restore to snailhouse fold and proceed with marking. Unlike the basic elephant's foot, this design requires marking snailhouses (RO) on only one side of the folded overlay. The incision lies ⅞" from the center of the overlay. The center of the circle lies ⅞" from the right fold. The circle is 1¼" in diameter.	*Corners (Finish):* Mark points 1¾" and 2⅜" from the outer edge measuring along both diagonal folds. For inverted saw-toothed finish, mark points ⅞" from the unfinished outer edge.
		Precutting Completely cut the snailhouses. Cut no more than ⅛" snips along the folds to indicate the rings.
		Postcutting After the snailhouses have been stitched, cut and stitch the rings and corners according to the photograph.
	Note: The center of the circle should	**Finish** Inverted sawtooth (see Finishes).

RH-1: Rams' Heads — Square Dance in the Barnyard

RH-1

Fold

Two-step marking

Rams' Heads — Square Dance in the Barnyard.

Snailhouse.

Both sides are identical with RO and LO rams' heads. For the RO ram's head, the base begins ¼″ from the center of the overlay and is ⅞″ in length. The junction lies on a line 1⅝″ from the center of the overlay. The center of the circle lies ⅝″ from the right-hand fold. The circle is ¹⁵⁄₁₆″ in diameter. For the LO ram's head, the base begins 4½″ from the center of the overlay and is ⅞″ in length. The junc-

tion lies on a line 3⅛″ from the center of the overlay. The center of the circle lies ⅝″ from the left-hand fold. The circle is ¹⁵⁄₁₆″ in diameter.

Fence: 2⅜″ from the center of the overlay.

Precutting

Completely cut the rams' heads, using the procedures for right and left orientation. Cut two ½″ slashes for the fence.

Postcutting

Use a marker and a ruler (or your thumbnail) to draw the remaining portions of the fence. Cut and stitch.

Finish

Inverted sawtooth (see Finishes).

RH-2: Rams' Heads and Snailhouses

RH-2	Ram's Heads and Snailhouses.	incision lies 3½ ″ from the center of the overlay. The center of the circle lies ⅞ ″ from the diagonal fold. The circle is 1⅛ ″ in diameter.
Fold	Snailhouse.	
Two-part marking	Both sides are identical with an RO ram's head and an LO snailhouse. For the RO ram's head, the base begins ¼ ″ from the center of the overlay and is ½ ″ in length. The junction lies on a line 1¾ ″ from the center of the overlay. The center of the circle lies ¾ ″ from the diagonal fold. The circle is 1⅛ ″ in diameter. For the LO snailhouses, the	

Precutting Completely cut the ram's head and snailhouses.

Postcutting The partial fence must be postcut because the segments do not meet at the foldlines. The corner slashes must also be postcut.

Finish Simple (see Finishes).

RH-3: Rams and Rings

RH-3	Rams and Rings.	
Fold	Snailhouse/Star.	
Complex marking	Temporarily fold along the V/H axes, basting if necessary (see Basic Elephant's Foot). On the V/H fold, mark rings 2″ and 2½″ from the center of the overlay and snip ⅟₁₆″. Also mark the base of the "mountains" 3⅛″ from the center of the overlay, making a cut 1″ deep and parallel to the outer edge of the overlay. Restore to snailhouse fold and proceed with marking.	

Both sides of the overlay will be marked with RO and LO rams' heads. For the RO ram's head, the base begins ¼″ from the center of the overlay and is ¾″ in length. The junction lies on a line 1½″ from the center of the overlay. The center of the circle lies ⅝″ from the diagonal fold. The circle is ⅞″ in diameter. For the LO ram's head, the base begins 4⅞″ from the center of the overlay and is 1″ in length. The junction lies on a line 3⅝″ from the center of the overlay. The center of the circle lies ⅞″ from the diagonal fold. The circle is ⅞″ in diameter.

Rings: 2″ and 2½″ from the center of the overlay.

Precutting — Completely cut the rams' heads before you cut the rings. Precut no more than ⅟₁₆″ to ⅛″ for the rings.

Postcutting — Stitch all of the rams' heads before you cut the rings. The rings should lie ⅜″ apart. The mountains that lie on the V/H folds must be postcut, ½″ in total height.

Finish — Simple (see Finishes).

H-1: Hearts and Rings

H-1	Hearts and Rings.		of the overlay.
Fold	Snailhouse.	**Precutting**	Completely cut the hearts. Cut the
Two-step	Both sides are identical with RO		spiral with three inner rings so that the
marking	hearts.* For the RO hearts, the point		channels of the spiral will match the

Both sides are identical with RO hearts.* For the RO hearts, the point begins ⅜″ from the center of the overlay. The center of the spiral lies on a line 2¼″ from the center of the overlay. The center of the circle lies ⅞″ from the left diagonal fold. The circle is 1⅜″ in diameter.

Rings: 2¾″ and 3⅛″ from the center

Precutting Completely cut the hearts. Cut the spiral with three inner rings so that the channels of the spiral will match the channels between the outer rings.

Postcutting Cut and stitch the rings, one segment at a time.

Finish Simple (see Finishes).

Embellishment Diamonds (see Embellishments).

*The basic rules of orientation do not apply for hearts. See Basic Heart instructions.

H-2: Broken Hearts

H-2 **Fold** **Two-step** **marking**	Broken Hearts. Snailhouse. Both sides are identical with RO hearts.* For the RO hearts, the point lies ⅜″ from the center of the overlay. The center of the spiral lies on a line 2½″ from the center of the overlay. The center of the circle lies 1⅛″ from the left diagonal fold. The circle is 1½″ in diameter. The rim of the circle should lie ⅜″ from the diagonal fold. *Base of bar:* 1¼″ from center of overlay.	**Precutting** **Postcutting** **Finish**	Completely cut the hearts. For the bar, cut a ⅜″ base perpendicular to the diagonal fold. Stitch the hearts except where they will overlap the bars. The cutting line for the bar will intersect the outermost channel of the spiral (see photograph). The total length of the cutting line for the bar is 3¼″. Cut and stitch the bars in 1″ segments to minimize distortion. Simple (see Finishes).

*The basic rules of orientation do not apply for hearts. See Basic Heart instructions.

H-3: Hearts All Around

H-3	Hearts All Around.
Fold	Snailhouse.
Two-step marking	Both sides are identical, with a RO and LO heart on each.* For the RO heart, the point begins ¼″ from the center of the overlay. The center of the spiral lies on a line 2″ from the center of the overlay. The center of the circle lies ¾″ from the left diagonal fold. The circle is 1¼″ in diameter. For the LO heart, the point begins 5¼″ from the

center of the overlay. The center of the spiral lies on a line 3½″ from the center of the overlay. The center of the circle lies ¾″ from the right diagonal fold. The circle is 1¼″ in diameter.

Precutting	Completely cut all the hearts. No precutting for the quadrant corners is possible.
Postcutting	Quadrant corners.
Finish	Simple (see Finishes).

*The basic rules of orientation do not apply for hearts. See Basic Heart instructions.

H-4: Inverted Hearts with Plumes

H-4	Inverted Hearts with Plumes.*
Fold	Snailhouse.
Two-step marking	Both sides are identical with LO hearts (point of heart lies 3⅞″ from the center of the overlay). The center of the spiral lies on a line 2¼″ from the center of the overlay. The center of the circle lies ¾″ from the right-hand fold. The circle is 1″ in diameter.

Point of ring: 4¼″ from the center of the overlay.

Plume: ⅜″ from the center of the overlay. The tip is ½″ long.

Precutting	Completely cut the hearts.
Postcutting	After the hearts are stitched, cut and stitch the plumes with the associated rings, which lie ¼″ outside of the hearts.
Finish	Double sawtooth (see Finishes).
Embellishment	Reverse-appliquéd squares (see Embellishments).

*The basic rules of orientation do not apply for hearts. See Basic Heart instructions.

H-5: Hearts and Star

H-5	Hearts and Star.
Fold	Snailhouse/Star.
Complex	Temporarily fold along the V/H axes,
marking	basting if necessary (see Basic Elephant's Foot). On the V/H axes, mark and snip the points of the star 1⅜″ and 1⅞″ from the center of the overlay. Make similar snips on the diagonal fold. Restore to snailhouse fold and proceed with marking.

Both sides are identical with LO hearts.* For the LO heart, the point lies 4½″ from the center of the overlay. The center of the spiral lies on a line 2⅞″ from the center of the overlay. The center of the circle lies ¾″ from the right-hand fold. The circle is 1⅛″ in diameter.

Point of ring: 5″ from the center of the overlay.

Precutting	Completely cut the hearts.
Postcutting	After the hearts are stitched, cut the rings ⅜″ outside the hearts. Along the V/H folds, cut the channels for the bars, then stitch the bars and outer channel of the star as one continuous channel. Cut and stitch the inner star channel.
Finish	Simple (see Finishes).

*The basic rules of orientation do not apply for hearts. See Basic Heart instructions.

Rich in color, this 86"×106" coverlet combines the *Lotus* design with dragons' tail motifs in the secondary borders, all couched in gold to produce an elegant example of pa ndau appliqué. Compare this exquisite piece with the other version of *Lotus* shown in this color section. *Author's collection.*

This collection of designs illustrates graphic use of color. Clockwise from upper left are the *Star and Snailhouses* (two-color background); asymmetrical *Snailhouses* (two-color background); *Elephant's Foot* (two-color background); the whimsical and oversimplified *Dragon's Tail* (effective use of appliquéd embellishment); and in the center, a Rainbow Star (strip-pieced background). Squares are 9″ to 12″ in size. The hearts may be used to adorn a pocket, a purse, or even a napkin ring. *Author's collection.*

This fine 19″×19″ *Elephant's Foot* exemplifies the exquisite embroidery used to embellish pa ndau appliqué. The peacock's eyes are $\frac{5}{16}$″ long, the satin stitch triangles have $\frac{1}{16}$″ bases, and rows of tiny running stitches follow the rings and channels of the intricate reverse-appliquéd border. *Author's collection.*

Pa ndau appliqué fits into any decor! The design in the 90″×105″ coverlet is a simple arrangement of dragons' tails, yet the subtle coloring combined with lavish adornment of appliquéd diamonds produces an icy, shimmering effect. The 24″×24″ wall hanging is an exceptional example of the cucumber motif. *Author's collection.*

The vest, traditionally worn by both men and women to New Year's festivities and on other special occasions, is decorated with strips of 3″-wide snailhouse pairs and appliquéd triangles that are ⅛″ wide at the base. Adding a festive jingle are the tin "coins," symbolic of real coins used in times past to indicate the wealth of the wearer. The motif on the hat indicates that it belongs to a boy. *Author's collection.*

The intrinsic beauty of pa ndau appliqué lies in its symmetry, but the *Leaf*, a popular traditional design, is the exception to the rule. The subtle color combination in this 19″×19″ piece is enlivened by the gold couching along the zigzag edges of the veins and stems of the leaf. *Author's collection.*

This fascinating 44″×48″ piece follows a classic color scheme, but its triangle borders are non-traditional. First, the width of the three triangle borders varies; second, the colors of the triangles are mixed; and third, the outer two triangle borders are not separated by a secondary border. The width of the secondary borders and the size of the appliquéd diamonds also vary. *Author's collection.*

This 24"×24" *Lotus* wallhanging is typical of the traditional style, both in border design and color. *Author's collection.*

This unique design entwines the ram's head, elephant's foot, and heart motifs so artistically that no single element is dominant. The arrows, pointing both inward and outward, create movement that enhances the captivating quality of the 6½"×6½" piece. *Author's collection.*

A complex arrangement of motifs and borders effectively combines the colors of earth and sky in an extraordinary, 108″×132″ summer coverlet. The basic design is a checkerboard of snailhouses and fletches (arrow feathers), both of which are repeated in the secondary borders. The diamond borders, less common than the simpler triangle borders, add a finishing touch of distinction to this perfectly executed pa ndau piece. *Courtesy of Katy Hoover.*

Party guests gather, sporting vests finished with pa ndau. The design on the vest at far left is cut directly into the garment. All other vests shown are appliquéd, then either machine- or hand-quilted, or left without batting for lightweight summer wear. Embellishments include rickrack, purchased bias tape, and eyelet lace. The child in the center is wearing the traditional Hmong party costume.

4 Foundation-Cut Designs

There are a handful of pa ndau appliqué designs that are created entirely by foundation cutting. This is because the design would require complex folding and refolding, layers far too thick to allow precision cutting, or precutting that would result in unmanageable distortion of the overlay. Even though a few helpful guidelines could be precut for some of these designs, the time and trouble of folding and prebasting outweigh any minute advantage precut markings could offer. The designs are cut into the overlay a segment at a time, after the three layers have been stacked and basted. Lines of symmetry may be marked with the thumbnail (Hmong method) or with a washable marker (American method). Then addi-tional guidelines are added for each specific motif.

The issue of construction causes these designs to be assigned to this chapter; they are all foundation-cut. Visually, however, they may belong in one of the standard categories. If so, a notation has been included.

Cucumber Seed. The cucumber seed is actually a primary motif. Not only is it easily recognizable, it is popular with the Hmong. The *Cucumber Seed* requires the skill of an expert. The outer ellipse is marked, cut, and stitched first. Then the inner channel is cut and stitched an inch or two at a time. The motif is also used in repeats as an allover design and is a popular center motif.

Foundation Cut 1: *Cucumber Seed* (primary motif)

Foundation Cut 2: *Froglegs* (allover design)

Froglegs is a well-known pattern among Hmong needle artists, but few are eager to undertake it. You begin by marking off a 25 unit × 25 unit grid on the foundation-basted overlay. The outermost channel, with its four U's at the midpoints of the sides, is the best place to begin the elaborate process of cutting and stitching. The next channel toward the center is simply an echo of the first channel. Then the fun begins! Trace the design with a pencil point, and see if *you* can find a simple way to go about it.

Foundation Cut 3: Maze (allover design)

Maze. The Maze is equally as challenging as the cucumber seed motif. *For this design, it is recommended that you completely stitch the outer edge before cutting any of the design.* Establish the diagonal lines of symmetry and four additional lines that connect the midpoints of the sides of the overlay. Begin cutting at the center. Cut around Subunit 1 and stitch the side of the channel that belongs to that subunit. Then cut around Subunit 2 and stitch. Separate and stabilize each of the square and triangular subunits before you begin cutting the inner mazes. Obviously, the design falls into the allover category.

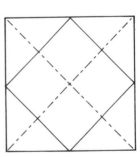

Guidelines for Maze, Spinning Wheel, and Saw-toothed Squares

Foundation Cut 4: Radiating Sawtooth (allover design)

Radiating Sawtooth. The radiating sawtooth design actually has no name; it is simply row after row of the sawtooth finish used around the outer edges of pa ndau appliqué overlays. Mark equidistant lines parallel to the lines that join the midpoints of the sides of the overlay. Follow the instructions for sawtooth finish for cutting and stitching (see Finishing). This is another allover design.

Guidelines for radiating saw-toothed rows

Foundation Cut 5: *Spinning Wheel* (primary motif)

Spinning Wheel. In the old country, nearly every home had a spinning wheel. Therefore, this pa ndau appliqué design is well known, even if few ever attempt it. This design could be easily precut into a star or snailhouse fold, but the cutting is so simple and the risk of distortion so great that foundation cutting is recommended.

Mark both diagonals and the lines that connect the midpoints of the sides of the overlay. Cut and stitch the innermost channels first, then create the outer channels. A few quick measurements and markings will ensure success.

Foundation Cut 6: Saw-toothed Squares (allover design)

Saw-toothed Squares. Because of its strong visual impact, the last of the foundation-cut designs deserves a special name; yet it has no name. Though it has been called Navaho Blanket, that name is entirely inappropriate. And to call it "god's eye" implies symbolism that probably does not exist. (Here we have a splendid example of the frustrations of Hmong nomenclature and symbolism.) Therefore, a purely functional name, Saw-toothed Squares, has been given to this allover design.

Mark, cut, and stitch the outer edges of the twelve subunits as indicated for the Maze. Then add the saw-toothed edge to the inside of each square and triangle. The cross is last to be cut and stitched. (See Foundation 6.)

Because all of these designs require skill and patience, they are designated "for experts only."

5 Mastering Geometric Design Analysis

Many variations and combinations of pa ndau designs are largely self-explanatory. They are included here, without instructions, so that you may practice analyzing the designs on your own.

Exercises in Design. Examine the photograph of each design and decide which lines of symmetry must be cut.

Then use your sewing and knitting gauge and circle stencil to determine the marking specifications for each design. Cut the markings into a paper "overlay" and compare your results with the photograph, paying careful attention to orientation. One hint: do not try to cut an entire design — it will fall into your lap in small motifs!

Proper category assignments and suggestions for folding appear at the end of the chapter.

Design Exercise 1.

Design Exercise 2. *Courtesy of Kathleen Pease.*

Design Exercise 3.

Design Exercise 4.

Design Exercise 5.

Design Exercise 6.

Design Exercise 7.

Design Exercise 8.

Complex designs

The basic instructions for the elephant's foot motif taught the concept of complex marking and cutting. For that motif, simplification would be easy to accomplish. By precutting only the snailhouse pairs and leaving the rings for the postcutting stage, only the snailhouse fold would be required. As you go through these exercises, remember that, in some designs, complex marking and cutting are not a matter of choice, but of necessity. Designs that have spiraling motifs often fall into this category because no more than four layers of fabric can be accurately cut at one time. Designs with asymmetrical motifs usually require complex cutting as well.

To practice the process, work through these instruc-

tions for complex Double-Symmetry Snailhouses.

Double-Symmetry Snailhouses

Fold	The overlay will eventually be folded into the pinwheel fold.
Complex marking and precutting	Fold the overlay according to Step 1 of the pinwheel. Prebaste. Fold along the vertical axis. Lightly prebaste, using a second color of basting thread. Mark two RO snailhouses — one on the vertical fold and one on the horizontal fold. The incision lies 2¼″ from the center of the overlay. The center of the circle lies ⅞″ from the fold. The cir-

Double-Symmetry Snailhouses (complex design)

cle is 1⅜″ in diameter. Completely precut the snailhouses. Remove the second set of basting stitches (easily recognized by color).

Fold the overlay according to the final step of the pinwheel fold. Prebaste. Mark two LO snailhouses, one on each diagonal fold. The incision lies 3⅝″ from the center of the overlay. The center of the circle lies ⅝″ from the fold. The circle is 1⅛″ in diameter. Completely precut the snailhouses.

Foundation basting and stitching Extensive foundation basting will be necessary. Stitch the eight snailhouse pairs in any order you wish.

Finish Simple (see Finishes).

Embellishment Diamonds (see Embellishments).

These helpful hints should aid you in your exercises in design analysis.

Design Exercise 1: Variation; snailhouse fold.

Design Exercise 2: Variation; snailhouse fold (center *could* be cut on star fold).

Design Exercise 3: Complex (center cobweb) or variation. Center can be cut on star fold, but snailhouses require snailhouse fold.

Design Exercise 4: Combination (complex if an extra fold is added so that N-S-E-W snailhouses can be precut); snailhouse fold.

Design Exercise 5: Variation; snailhouse fold.

Design Exercise 6: Combination; snailhouse fold (RO snailhouse on one side only, LO heart on both sides).

Design Exercise 7: Variation; snailhouse fold.

Design Exercise 8: Complex; star and snailhouse folds.

Unit IV The Finishing Touches

1 Finishes for the Overlay

Like a frame on a painting, the finish used on a pa ndau appliqué piece should complement the design. However, unlike a frame, the finish for the pa ndau piece must be determined in the earliest stages of design, with virtually no chance for alteration.

There are six popular finishes for the edges of an overlay. These general rules apply to all of them.

- In most cases, you should make only a tiny snip in the prebasted overlay.
- A ¼″ snip into the diagonal fold will result in a corner cut, and a small cut into the V/H fold will result in a straight cut parallel to the edge in the center of each side. In either V/H or diagonal folds, these snips are made parallel to the outer edge of the overlay. (The only exception to this rule is the Double Sawtooth Finish.)
- The measurements for finishes are usually *the distance from the marking to the outer edge* and *not* the distance from the center, as it is for all other design specifications. For marking, do not place the ruler alongside the diagonal fold. Instead, lay it perpendicular to the outer edge.
- Always baste the outer edge when you foundation baste the design.
- Completely stitch the design before beginning any postcutting or stitching on the outer edges.
- Always appliqué one side of a strip before you postcut the second side. For example, for single channel, stitch the outer edge before you cut the channel. Then stitch the *inner* side of the channel as you postcut. With this technique, a strip of fabric will never be permitted to "float."

Simple finish. The simple finish is the easiest to execute and has the least impact upon the central design of the piece. The edge of the overlay is turned under and stitched after all of the design has been completed. No precutting or postcutting is necessary. The motifs

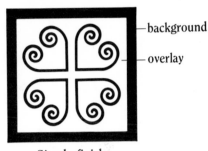

— background
— overlay

Simple finish

may extend as close as ½″ from the cut edge of the overlay. (See S-2.)

Channel finish. The channel finish is also easily precut and stitched. Precut snips in the diagonal and/or V/H fold ⅝″ from the cut edge of the overlay. This allows a ¼″ seam along the outer edge, a ³⁄₁₆″ turn-under along the channel, and a ³⁄₁₆″ strip remaining as a frame for the piece. Always stitch the entire outer edge before you cut the fabric along the channel. Cut only a 1″ segment at a time and stitch the *inner* edge first. This minimizes potential distortion. Particular attention to precision at the corners ensures a pleasing effect. (See SH-2.)

background

Channel finish

Double channel finish. The double channel finish occupies considerable space and provides a substantial, yet understated, finish to the outer edge. Precut ⅝″ and 1″ from the outer edge into the V/H and/or diagonal folds. For maximum stability, stitch the five cut edges in the order indicated in the diagram. (See S-1.)

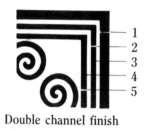

Double channel finish

Sawtooth finish. On a piece in which the overlay is 8″ to 9″ square, the distance from the stitched outer edge to the flat edge of the sawtooth channel should be a minimum of ¾″. *Notice that the postcut line is off-center in relation to the two flat edges of the finish to allow for notching.* Therefore, the initial precutting into the V/H and diagonal folds should be approximately ⅞″ from the cut edge of the overlay. Stitch the outer edge. Postcut and stitch the flat side of the channel along all four sides in 1″ segments, cutting as indicated by the dotted line in the diagram. Then cut triangles out of the remaining fabric for the saw-toothed edge. (See the Templates and Tools chapter for instructions on making all of the triangles the same size.)

The amount of background that shows between the tips of the triangles and the flat side of the channel depends on the amount of seam allowance that is turned under. The wider the seam allowance, the more visible the background. Along the flat side, you may decide to turn under a scant ⅛″ seam allowance, reducing the amount of visible background. An expert will allow the balance of color to be a deciding factor as she deter-

mines the proper width of the saw-toothed finish. (See EF-4 for an example of this finish.)

Inverted sawtooth finish. This finish is also the result of an off-center cutting line in the channel. In this case, however, the cutting is closer to the outer edge than one would expect — approximately ⅝″ for an overlay of 8″ to 9″. Stitch the outer edge, then cut and stitch the flat side of the channel in short segments. Cut and stitch the notched edge according to the instructions for the simple sawtooth finish, creating pointed corners as indicated in the diagram. (See RH-1.)

Inverted sawtooth finish

Double sawtooth finish. The precutting for this finish is different from the rest. Make a snip *perpendicular to the diagonal fold*. It should lie ⅞″ from the outer edge (1¼″ along the diagonal). After stitching the outer edge, zigzag-cut and stitch triangles along one side of the channel, a few triangles at a time. Two markings might be helpful: a lightly marked baseline ⅝″ from the stitched outer edge, and a series of equally spaced dots marked so that the triangles will all be the same size. Each corner is a single channel that is cut along the diagonal axis. (See H-2.)

These finishes may all be used along the outer edge of the overlay. When used in combinations, they become intriguing secondary motifs that can be alternated with other motifs to form marvelous echo patterns.

Sawtooth finish

Double sawtooth finish

Snailhouses and Radiating Saw-Toothed Rows: In this 34″×34″ piece, rows of the sawtooth finish are used to create an echo effect. No borders or embellishments have been included. *Author's collection.*

In this 16″×16″ Heart and Rings design, the sawtooth finish and the zigzag arrows in the center and corners create a pleasing, well-balanced piece. The relatively wide channel of the dragon's tail ring emphasizes the circular nature of the design. *Author's collection.*

2 Embellishments

After all the reverse appliqué is completed and the edges are stitched, the piece is ready for those wonderful finishing touches that add interest and balance to the overall design. These bits of artistry give the piece its individuality, its spark. They may take the form of simple appliqués, embroidery, postcut reverse appliqué, or a combination of these techniques.

To add appliqués, cut the motifs from fabrics, baste them in place, then secure them with appliqué stitch. For a few shapes, such as the petals of *Water Lily*, you may wish to cut the appliqué from a square of fabric folded into quarters, or even into a star fold. This will produce a symmetrical appliqué.

The embroidery should be extremely fine, stitched in bright, clear colors. The channels of stars and spirals are often embroidered with running stitches or backstitches along their midlines. This gives the appearance of true quilting, and is often mistaken as such by the casual observer. The couched herringbone stitch is popular for the wide borders that often surround the pa ndau appliqué design. Embroidered stars and satin-stitched, tiny triangles or peacock eyes are often sprinkled across the pa ndau appliqué piece like candies and sugar on cookies. For more information on these embroidery stitches, refer to the Bibliography.

Center diamonds

Center diamonds

Square peg in a round hole

Appliqué

Diamond

Water lily

Pinwheel

Appliqué

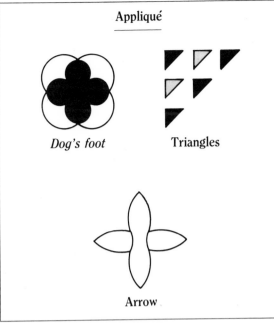

Dog's foot

Triangles

Arrow

Reverse Appliqué

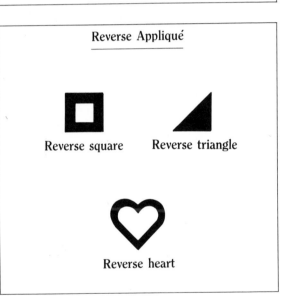

Reverse square

Reverse triangle

Reverse heart

Embroidery

Satin stitch

Combination

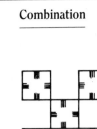

Appliquéd squares with satin stitch

Star stitch

Cucumber Seed

Backstitch
(used along midline of channel)

- - - - - - - - - -

Running stitch
(used along midline of channel)

Peacock Eye
(fishbone stitch surrounded by chain stitch)
actual size = ¼″

Couched herringbone stitch

3 Borders

Many of the pa ndau pieces that range in size from 10″ to 36″ consist of one central, reverse-appliquéd design surrounded by a series of borders. In nearly every piece, one border will have neatly spaced appliquéd triangles that are suggestive of mountains. These borders are nearly always alternated with secondary borders, which command less attention and add "weight" to the piece. Secondary borders may be plain strips of fabric or ones embellished with embroidery, reverse appliqué, or another appliquéd motif. The borders themselves are usually edged on both sides by tiny strips of fabric that look like rows of piping.

If you wish to border your pa ndau appliqué piece, do not finish the outer edge of the overlay. Cut two strips of uniform width that are as long as the top of the piece. With right sides together, stitch them along the top and

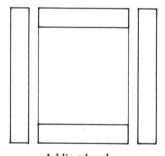

Adding borders

bottom edges of the appliqué, using a ¼″ seam. Then cut two more strips, the same width as the first, and long enough for the two sides. Stitch in place. Use this method for narrow strips (⅛″ to 1″ finished width), as well as for wide borders (1½″ to 4″). Allow additional width for seams.

The Hmong needle artists begin at the center, adding narrow strips and borders as fancy suits them. As these borders are stitched to one another, they are also stitched to the foundation layer of the central design.

When the outer edge of the foundation layer is reached, it is trimmed ½″ outside the last row of stitching, and the adding of borders continues. A lining is added to conceal the raw edges on the foundation layer.

Triangle borders. For a triangle border (sawtooth), add the four strips of background fabric according to the diagram. Divide the length of the side of the inner square into equal parts and determine the size and number of the triangles you will need, following the instructions in the chapter on templates. Draw a template and cut the triangles, adding a ⅛″ seam allowance.

To ensure proper placement, baste the triangles in place on one side of the square. The first and last triangle on each side should lie with its point exactly at the corner of the inner square. The midlines of these triangles should lie exactly in line with the adjoining sides

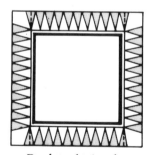

Border of triangles

of the inner square (see diagram). The seams joining the background strips will all be neatly hidden by the triangles that lie at the corners, but an irregular rectangle of background fabric will remain visible in each outer corner. The points of the triangles will barely touch the inner edge of the border. It is not necessary to turn under the seam allowance along the bases of the triangles, because they will be caught in the seam when the next border is joined.

Begin appliquéing one corner triangle and work toward the middle, stopping one or two triangles short of center. Then begin stitching triangles from the opposite end. In this way, the two or three triangles in the center will absorb any minor discrepancies. This is contrary to the usual practice of making the center perfect, but for a good reason. If the triangles that lie on the end are properly spaced and aligned, the irregularly shaped rectangles of background fabric will match on all four corners. If, on the other hand, the triangles do not fit at the corners, these unusual rectangles will become eyesores and detract from the impact of your work.

Occasionally, pa ndau pieces include a series of triangle borders that become progressively larger toward the outer edge. The triangle for each successive row is both taller and wider at the base than the triangle of the preceding border. In traditional Hmong pieces, the triangles may also be multicolored, creating a confetti-like effect. One wonderful example that combines both of these variations is featured on the Cover.

Narrow framing strips are often used in pairs on both sides of a triangle border. They usually are made from either the overlay or background fabric and an accent color.

Diamond borders. On large pieces, you may add a diamond border, the deluxe version of the triangle border, alternated with the secondary borders. Cut the border strips twice the width they would be for a triangle border (add seam allowances to both sides of each strip). Lightly mark a midline along the lengthwise dimension of the strip. Appliqué a row of triangles so that the points lie along the midline. Then stitch a second row of triangles along the second side, so that the points meet the points of the first row. Diamonds of background fabric will be formed between the tip-touching triangles. Because triangles lie along both seams of the border, the strip should be completed as a separate unit and then joined to the central portion. As the diagram indicates, the Hmong have not devised a convenient and appealing corner treatment for the diamond border.

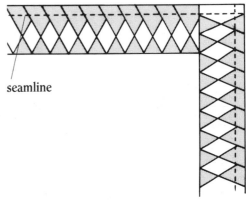

seamline

Border of diamonds

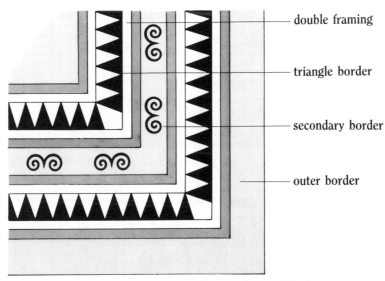

double framing

triangle border

secondary border

outer border

Borders and framing for pa ndau appliqué

This *Spiderweb* variation includes, in the usual proportions, borders typical of large pa ndau pieces. The dark framing strips emphasize the triangle borders, yet unify them with the central designs. The 66″×88″ piece could be used as a tablecloth, wall hanging, or summer quilt. *Author's collection.*

Secondary borders. Some designs are complemented best by quiet borders that offer the eye a rest. For example, border strips can be left plain. In the right color, the large empty space can add visual stability to a design. Embroidery is often used to enliven a large expanse that lacks interest. Sets of four or five appliquéd diamonds may also be used to adorn a single fabric border strip. Any one of these borders might be used alternately with borders of triangles to provide visual contrast, but in general, only one type of secondary border is used in a pa ndau piece. One final example, used particularly on large pieces, is the secondary border that consists of a series of small and evenly spaced reverse-appliqué motifs. To precut these, first mark the points at which

they can be precut with only one fold per motif and simple prebasting. For other motifs, such as a star or fletch, more difficult folds are usually required. You might consider doing a bit more postcutting to avoid so much folding and prebasting. For example, you might only square-fold the fabric for a star. Precut along the vertical and horizontal folds only, leaving the star points along the diagonal for thumbnail marking and postcutting.

Precutting border designs

If the foundation layer for the central design was not cut large enough for the borders, a new foundation or lining may be added at any point. This layer is especially beneficial for the borders of triangles, because additional stability helps the needle artist overcome the stretch of the triangles along their bias edges. Add this layer so that the right side will show in the finished piece.

dragon's tail   fletch

Reverse-appliquéd border motifs

the motifs are to be cut. Then fold and prebaste short sections according to the selected motif. Usually only a 4″ section of the strip is folded for each motif, so that the job is not so encumbering as it might seem. Snailhouse pairs are a popular motif for borders, and

Outer borders. They are usually plain, made with the darker color, and may be a bit wider than any of the other borders in the piece. This yields a weighty edge that constitutes a frame. If necessary, pin a lining in place, then turn under 1″ to 3″ of the outer edge and hem.

1 Garments and Pa nDau

Using pa ndau pieces on garments is an exciting way to work with small pieces that require less time and allow more experimentation with design and color. It also makes your artistry more visible to others.

There are two construction techniques for including pa ndau appliqué in garments. In the first, square designs are completed and appliquéd to a garment piece. For a professional finish, appliqué the pa ndau to the back of a vest, shirt, or jacket, and then line the garment. Or, purchase a garment and stitch a pa ndau piece on it. The second method is the most effective and the

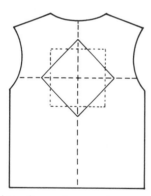

Establishing lines of symmetry on a garment

most difficult. With this technique, the design is cut directly into the garment piece so that the pa ndau becomes an integrated part of the garment. The difficulty lies in the size of the "overlay" and the fact that the garment is usually irregular in shape. The standard overlay is a square, with no right or left or top or bottom, so that the vertical and horizontal axes are identical. For a garment piece, however, you must first establish the vertical midline, determine the desired horizontal position, and then carefully fold and prebaste an irregularly shaped piece. For example, these are the construction techniques for a vest back.

For designs requiring square or star folds, follow these steps.

1 Fold the piece in half vertically and lightly crease. Snip the seam allowance along the fold at the top and bottom to make a permanent mark, using caution not to snip beyond the seamline. This establishes the vertical line of symmetry.

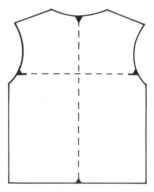

Indicate lines of symmetry by clipping the seam allowances.

2 Open the piece flat and, taking the size of your design into account, imagine how high on the piece it should lie. Mark the desired horizontal line of symmetry on one side, then refold the piece along the vertical midline and cut tiny snips in both sides at once to establish the horizontal line.

3 Due to the size of the garment piece, prebasting is best accomplished in two steps. With the piece folded in half vertically, baste along the midline and several inches into the piece. Then fold along the horizontal line and baste extensively. This step completes the square fold.

4 For the star fold, fold again, bringing the horizontal axis alongside the vertical axis. Prebaste.

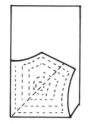

Square and star folds

For snailhouse folds or diagonally oriented squares and designs:

1 Carefully fold the piece (do not baste) according to the instructions for the star fold. Either iron in the creases along the diagonal foldlines or clip the seam allowances on the shoulders and sides.

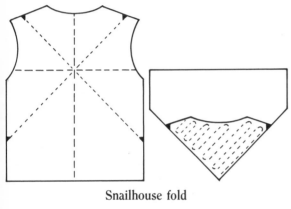

Snailhouse fold

2 Open the piece flat, then refold along the diagonals. Prebaste.

Designs that require other folds may be used, but the folding, prebasting, and precutting must be accomplished one section at a time. For a simple, single motif, such as a heart on a pocket, it may be necessary to make only one fold.

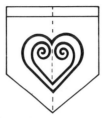

Simple pieces require one fold.

For mirror-image pieces, such as the yokes for a blouse or shirt, be careful to make the designs reflect one another accurately. Also, use a washable marker to note the right side of each garment piece and, if necessary, the "top right" and "top left" to differentiate between the vertical and horizontal axes.

One serious obstacle to the use of pa ndau appliqué in garment design is the limitation of fabric choices. Only tightly woven muslins or percales are suitable. On the other hand, while the fabrics may be plain, they can be enhanced with trimmings, piping, appliqué, and embroidery.

These mirror-image pieces do not reflect properly.

2   Templates and Tools

A template is a pattern — a simple tool that saves time, produces uniformity, and allows repeated use of the same design. The Hmong needle artists do not use templates when they create pa ndau appliqué designs. Few use anything as elementary as a ruler or a pencil. Their eyes are their guides; their thumbnails their marking utensils.

While many achieve incredible accuracy and uniformity, some would benefit from a few helpful tools. For the American needle artist who is accustomed to precision and control, those tools are essential. With no mother at your side to explain with her thumb and forefinger just how big to make a snailhouse, a simple ruler is a must.

Rulers

A clear plastic ruler with a ⅛″ grid is helpful for measuring and establishing lines that lie parallel to a fold, channel, or outer edge. The "sewing and knitting gauge" is a convenient 6″ long and has a useful feature, a sliding indicator. This indicator can be set at a particular measurement so that marking the distance along two or four foldlines can be accomplished quickly without errors or time spent rechecking instructions. Its real advantage is even greater. If the ends of the slide are laid gently and carefully alongside the fold, the ruler will be oriented perpendicular to the fold so that any marking made alongside the ruler will be on a line perpendicular to the fold. *This specification is used in all motifs that have a spiral as a component part.*

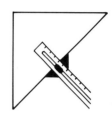

Establishing perpendicular lines

Circle stencils

Another valuable tool is the stencil for circles. The stencil is lightweight, clear plastic, with the circles cut out. The circles range from small to large and have tiny marks along the circumferences that indicate the two diameters that divide the circle into four quadrants. Imagine the two diameters that connect these markings — they cross in the center of the circle. After the center of a circle for a spiral has been marked, the circle stencil is laid in place so that imaginary diameters pass through the center marking. Then the circle, or rim of the spiral, is drawn. The stencils are available in a wide range of sizes and prices and may even include shapes other than circles. For the pa ndau appliqué designs in this book, you will need circles that range from ½″ to 1½″ in diameter.

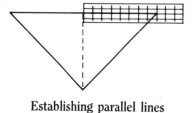

Establishing parallel lines

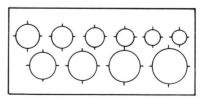

Circle stencil

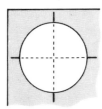

Quadrant marks indicate the center of the circle.

Templates

On occasion, you may wish to make several pieces from the same design and with a high degree of precision. This requires an accurate and fairly durable template. To make one, simply cut a piece of cardboard the size and shape of the prebasted overlay. Mark the specifications for the design on the cardboard *exactly as you would mark the prebasted fabric.*

The way in which you cut the design into the template depends upon the design itself. For a star, cut out slices of cardboard $\frac{1}{16}$″ in width or less at each marking. Cut

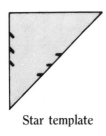

Star template

about $\frac{1}{4}$″ into the template. *Be careful that the angle of the cut is appropriate for the design.* Then, the next time you wish to cut the same design, just lay the template over the prebasted overlay and mark where the "slices" in the template appear.

To make a template for a RO snailhouse, cut a $\frac{1}{16}$″ slice in the cardboard along the incision, then cut out a generous one-half of the circle (see diagram). Mark-

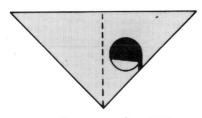

Snailhouse template (RO)

ing the incision and a portion of the rim should be adequate for snailhouses; to cut more out of the template would weaken it unnecessarily. To mark the RO snailhouse on the second side, flip the fabric over and begin again. A convenient reminder on the template to "mark on right fold only" will save time and frustration next time you cut the design. For LO snailhouses, cut the template along the left side.

With some designs, it will be difficult to know which point of the triangular template is the center of the overlay. A good example is a template that includes both RO and LO rams' heads. Notice in the diagram that the LO ram's head lies farther in from the outside point to allow a hem along the outer edge, while the RO lies

Non-reversible template

very near the inside point of the overlay. This template could be flipped, rotated, and used incorrectly. Therefore, it is a non-reversible template. Mark an X on the right side to indicate the center of the overlay.

Always match the template very precisely with the center of the prebasted overlay. A thorough job of prebasting is necessary if the templates are expected to yield a high degree of accuracy. Of course, the fewer markings you need, the easier it will be to make a useful template. For some designs and motifs, such as hearts, the template would be very fragile and the risk of distortion so great that the use of a template may actually be more time-consuming and frustrating than the straightforward marking of the overlay itself. Experience will be your best teacher.

Templates for appliquéd triangles

Making border strips with appliquéd triangles is greatly simplified if you make a template for the triangles. Experiment with this method, using a sheet of typing paper instead of fabric. Fold the paper in half ($4\frac{1}{4}$″ × 11″) and then in quarters ($2\frac{1}{8}$″×11″). Cut the paper into four strips along the foldlines. Fold one strip in half ($2\frac{1}{8}$″×$5\frac{1}{2}$″). Open the paper flat again and mark off a point 4″ from the midline on both ends. The following steps will determine the proper size of a template for a 2⅛″-wide border strip that will adjoin a design with an 8″ side.

1 Fold the paper along the midline again, matching the two pencil markings.
2 Fold the paper so that the midline is aligned with the pencil markings.
3 Turn the folded edge of the paper over to meet the midline. The paper now measures 2⅛″×2½″.
4 On the left side are the two ends of the strip. Fold these *back* at the pencil lines so that the paper measures 2⅛″×1½″.
5 Hold the paper tightly on the X and cut along the diagonal line, as shown in the diagram. The triangles that remain in your hand (the X side of the diagonal line) are the proper size and number for your border. Discard the other triangles and end pieces.

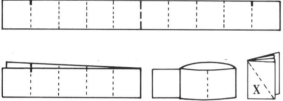

Determining the template for a triangle border

6 To check your work, glue the border triangles on one of the extra 2⅛″×11″ strips of paper. Determine the midline, then glue a center triangle in place, matching its midline to the midline of the border strip. Then glue two triangles to the right and two to the left of the center triangle. The border strip should be 8″ from the tip of the left triangle to the tip of the right triangle. The bases of the triangles are actually 10″ across.

Use any one of the triangles as an "actual size" template. As you draw around the template, you are marking sewing lines. Seam allowances must be added.

This same procedure can be used to make a triangle template for a border of any size. Simply cut a strip of paper (use freezer or wrapping paper for long borders)

to the proper width and 3″ to 5″ longer than the side of the square to which the border is to be joined. Determine the midline, mark the desired length of the strip to the right and left of the midline, and fold as explained above until the paper is small enough for just half of

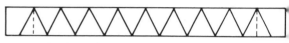

Checking the accuracy of the template

one triangle. Personal judgment and choice will determine when you have folded enough. This method will always produce an odd number of triangles. When you appliqué them, one should sit right in the center of the border, and the tips of the two end triangles should always point toward the inner corner of the central square.

The triangles will be long and thin or short and plump depending upon the width of the strip and the number of folds you choose to make. Experiment with paper and scissors until you feel comfortable with the procedure. For long border strips, you may eliminate bulk and achieve the same result by folding and cutting a paper strip one-half the desired length, plus 3″ to 5″. In this case you will match the midline of the strip with one endpoint instead of matching the two endpoints for the first fold. You may go one step further and use a *quarter* of a strip if you feel extremely confident with this method.

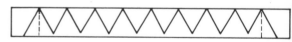

Slightly skew cut produces chain of triangles

Note: If you cut a slightly imperfect diagonal, the triangles will be connected like paper dolls. The resulting template will be ever so slightly imperfect, but you will have a lovely continuous string of triangles to check your accuracy.

3 Unconventional Concepts In Color and Design

The overwhelming majority of pa ndau appliqué pieces have a single background fabric. The designs are, therefore, two-colored, with the possible addition of accent colors in the embellishment. In a few pieces, however, motifs appear in more than one color. It is difficult to say whether this is traditional or just a new twist in response to America's fascination with the molas of the San Blas Indians. Probably, it is safe to assume that if the variegated background were truly traditional, we would see far more examples of it.

If you wish to use more than one background color, precut and baste the layers together as usual. Then stitch the motifs that are to appear in the basic background color. Remove the basting and insert pieces of the second background color wherever you like. Baste and stitch the remaining motifs. With this method, each entire motif will appear in one color, but the overall design will be multicolored. For very simple designs, you may be able to insert pieces of the second background color as you initially layer the fabrics for foundation basting. Or, for small corner motifs, you may be able to insert the small pieces of secondary background through the opening created by the precutting, thereby eliminating the need to remove the basting along the outer edge of the overlay.

Nontraditional star

A second method of achieving background color variation is much simpler, but much less exacting. Simply machine-piece (or hand-stitch) strips of fabric together on the diagonal. Use this composite as the background. In this way, a single motif may appear in several colors, depending on the number of splicings in the background layer. Examples of this technique appear in the Color Section.

Another possibility is that of ever-widening channels or strips. The Hmong definitely do not do this, but it would be an interesting thing to try on your own.

Inserting a second background color

Multicolored effect

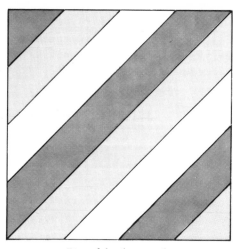

Pieced background

4 "Summer Quilts" and Wall Hangings

Lightweight pa ndau appliqué pieces, stitched together, can make an unusual "summer quilt." If your stitching is meticulous, the bedcovering will be durable despite the narrow seam allowances.

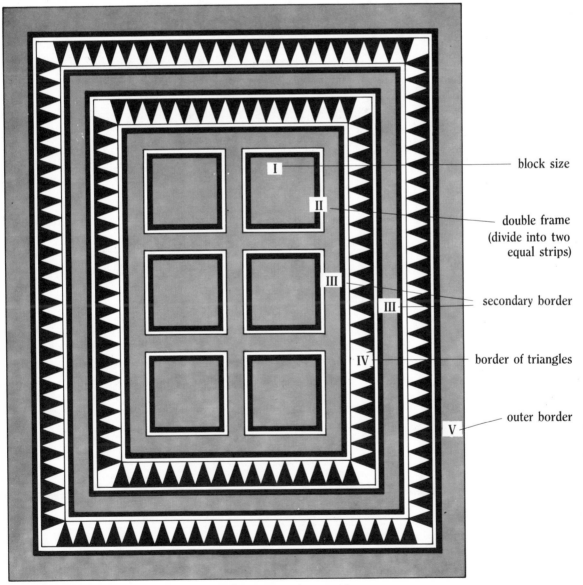

block size

double frame
(divide into two
equal strips)

secondary border

border of triangles

outer border

Full or queen-size coverlet

Wall hanging

Determine the appropriate number of design blocks for your bed size. To each block, add a double frame, consisting of two fabrics that are identical in width. These are joined one color at a time (¼″ seam allowance) to the design block. Traditional Hmong pieces do not have mitered corners (welcome relief for many of us). Cut two short and two longer strips from each of the two fabrics. Then join the framed blocks together with lattice strips to form the central portion of the bedcovering.

When this stage has been completed, add a lining. Lay out a piece of fabric (pieced if necessary) that is 10″ larger in each direction than the joined blocks. Carefully center the blocks on it and baste in place. Sew double framing strips to the central piece, stitching through to the lining at the same time. All of the straight seams of the borders and frames should penetrate the lining.

Set the center portion aside and begin the individual triangle (sawtooth) strips. Pin the end triangles in place to guarantee proper placement, but do not stitch them until the four strips have been joined to the main section. The tips of the triangles should lie precisely ¼″ from the cut edge of the strip, and the ends of the triangles will overlap slightly at the bottom. A sharp V

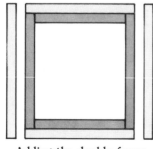

Adding the double frame

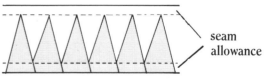

Proper position for the triangles

seam allowance

110

should lie between each pair of triangles exactly ¼" from the bottom edge. It is not necessary to turn under a seam allowance on the bases of the triangles. Join the strips to the central portion of the bedcovering, stitching through to the lining, and carefully stitching from triangle point to triangle point for a perfectly matched seam. Finish by appliquéing the end triangles over the seam allowance of the border strips.

The secondary borders (III) should be completed in the same manner. Add any appliquéd or reverse-appliquéd embellishment to the single strips, then join them to the central portion. Continue in this manner until all of the border strips are attached. Trim the lining 1½" inside the cut edge of the outer border. Turn under a ½" hem and stitch.

The lining has been attached along each frame and border seam. Tack it in place at several points in the central portion, as well.

The following basic dimensions and layout diagrams are all you need to create your own summer quilt.

For the full-size/queen-size coverlet, with a tuck-under allowance for the pillows, the dimensions for the design block and border strips are as follows:

I   (block)   = 13"
II (two-color framing)   = 2" total (1" + 1")
III (secondary border)   = 3"
IV (triangle border)   = 3"
V   (outer border)   = 4"

The blocks are arranged two across and three down. The finished size will be 85"×105".

This 34"×44" *Spiderweb* wall hanging has simplified borders. *Courtesy of Joy Neal Kidney.*

For the full-size bedspread, the dimensions for the design block and border strips are as follows:

I	(block)	=	12″
II	(two-color framing)	=	2″ total (1″ + 1″)
III	(secondary border)	=	3″
IV	(triangle border)	=	3″
V	(outer border)	=	4″

The blocks are arranged two across and three down. The finished size will be 91½″×112″.

For the king-size coverlet, with a tuck-under allowance for the pillows, the dimensions for the design block and border strips are as follows:

I	(block)	=	11″
II	(two-color framing)	=	2″ total (1″ + 1″)
III	(secondary border)	=	3″
IV	(triangle border)	=	3″
V	(outer border)	=	4″

The blocks are arranged three across and four down. The finished size will be 99″×117″. (You may eliminate the outer border on the top edge to reduce the lengthwise dimension.)

For the large wall hanging, strips of secondary border completely surround the two center blocks (see diagram). The following dimensions will produce a 53″×68″ piece.

I	(block)	=	10″
II	(two-color framing)	=	1½″ total (¾″ + ¾″)
III	(secondary border)	=	2″
IV	(triangle border)	=	3″
V	(outer border)	=	4″

For a smaller wall hanging, the secondary border strips that surround the central blocks in the previous example are omitted (see photograph). The following dimensions will produce a 34″×44″ wall hanging:

I	(block)	=	10″
II	(two-color framing)	=	¾″ total (⅜″ + ⅜″)
III	(secondary border)	=	2″
IV	(triangle border)	=	2″
V	(outer border)	=	3″

A few creative souls will want to use pa ndau appliqué in the great American format, the sampler quilt. The completed designs can be easily joined in rows with lat-ticework (sashing) and borders in the style of the traditional sampler quilt. Framing each pa ndau design with a narrow strip of a dark fabric will delineate the squares and lend uniformity to your very special summer sampler.

The *nyia* (knee-ah) is the official baby carrier of the Hmong. It is simply a flat, rectangular piece, elaborately decorated with pa ndau appliqué and embroidery and held in place by a binding. Pictured here is young Mung Moua with his mother Sao Thao Lee.

Photograph by Myron Miller, copyright 1983.

Glossary

Allover design — A design consisting of a single motif (primary or secondary) that is repeated as a basic unit.

Background layer — The layer of fabric that appears as the design in pa ndau appliqué.

Channel — The exposed section of background that forms the pa ndau design.

Color testing — Testing the dyes in fabric for color-fastness and removing any residual dyes.

Combination design — A design in which two or more distinct primary motifs are used; also, a design of secondary motifs, with no one dominant motif.

Complex design — A design that requires more than one fold and/or two-part basting; also, any design in which the primary motifs are so entwined that they are not distinct.

Decorative cutting — Cutting of secondary motifs or edges into the flat and foundation-basted overlay without the benefit of precutting. This is usually done after the primary design is completed (see foundation cutting).

Foundation basting — The basting that secures the three layers of pa ndau together.

Foundation cutting — The cutting of an entire design into the overlay after the layers are stacked and basted. This is usually done without precutting.

Foundation layer — The bottom, functional layer in pa ndau appliqué that provides stability during stitching and to the finished product.

Overlay — The top piece of fabric in pa ndau appliqué; the layer into which the design is cut.

Pa ndau — Any one of the needle art forms of Hmong folk art. Directly translated, the term means *flower cloth*.

Pa ndau appliqué — The needle art form of the Hmong that combines geometric cutting, reverse appliqué, and optional embellishment with embroidery or appliqué. Pronounced pond-ouw.

Postcutting — The cutting that completes a partially precut design after the three layers have been stacked and basted.

Prebasting — The basting of the folded overlay prior to cutting.

Precutting — The partial or complete cutting of a design into the prebasted overlay.

Primary motifs — The design elements of pa ndau appliqué that are readily recognized and dominate the overall design.

Reverse appliqué — A form of appliqué in which a design is cut out of the top layer of fabric, revealing an underlying background fabric.

Secondary motifs — The less distinct motifs that are used to complement the primary motifs in a design.

Segment — The portion of a design that is cut and stitched as a unit.

Simple design — A design that consists of one primary motif.

Strip — The section of overlay fabric that lies between two channels of the design.

Symmetry — The uniformity in size, shape, and relative position of design elements on opposite sides of a dividing line or about a center.

Variation — A design that has a primary motif and one or more secondary motifs.

V/H — The abbreviation for vertical axis/horizontal axis.

Bibliography

Garrett, W.E. "No Place to Run: The Hmong of Laos." *National Geographic* 1 (1974): 78–111.

Garrett, W.E. "Thailand: Refuge from Terror." *National Geographic* 5 (1980): 633–642.

Lartéguy, Jean, in collaboration with Yang Dao. *La Fabuleuse Aventure du Peuple de 1'Opium.* Paris: Presses de la Cite, 1979.

White, Peter T. "Mosaic of Cultures: The Lands and Peoples of Southeast Asia." *National Geographic* 3 (1971): 296–329.

White, Peter T. "The Mekong: River of Terror and Hope." *National Geographic* 12 (1968): 737–787.

Suggested Reading

For basic techniques

Hassel, Carla J. *You Can Be A Super Quilter: A Teach-Yourself Manual for Beginners.* Des Moines, Iowa: Wallace-Homestead Book Company, 1980.

For geometry and color information

Hassel, Carla J. *Super Quilter II: Challenges for the Super Quilter.* Des Moines, Iowa: Wallace-Homestead Book Company, 1982.

For embroidery instruction and information on molas

Gostelow, Mary. *A World of Embroidery.* New York: Charles Scribner's Sons, 1975.

Wilson, Erica. *Erica Wilson's Embroidery Book.* New York: Charles Scribner's Sons, 1973.

For children

Goldfarb, Mace. *Fighters, Refugees, Immigrants: A Story of the Hmong.* Minneapolis: Carolrhoda Books, 1982.

Index

Four-color photographs are indicated in boldface type.

Keeping Pa nDau Alive

In January, 1983, a project was initiated to create employment for the Hmong refugees in Des Moines, Iowa. Plans included a farm, a printing operation, a building maintenance service, and a sewing enterprise. Pa ndau, of course, would have been a natural for the sewing venture, but a prominent retail chain said they felt that pa ndau had no commercial potential. However, they were interested in purchasing "early American quilts." I was asked by the project director to coordinate the quilt business as a volunteer instructor. I said "yes, of course," thinking my biggest task would be to design quilts that would please the department store buyers and that could be made profitably by a cottage industry.

I knew none of the Hmong women spoke English, so I planned to learn enough of *their* language to translate sewing instructions and fabric and cutting requirements. Then, I thought, I would transcribe all the information into their language for future reference. This seemed like a simple plan. But what I didn't realize is that Hmong has only recently become a written language, and spelling and vocabulary are still terribly inconsistent. Furthermore, because the women are still not being educated and the men are oblivious to the skills and terminology required for fine needlework, simple instructions could not even be *translated*, let alone written.

Another obstacle was that, in the Hmong culture, younger people do not presume to teach older ones. No wonder the women asked my age the very day I walked in the door! Only the youngest women were conditioned to follow my instructions.

I began reading everything I could find about the Hmong — even a text written in French. I quickly learned that the Hmong were making incredible adjustments to a new language, a new religion, a new environment, a new culture, and new expectations. This would be difficult for any immigrant, but for these "free spirits" from the mountains of Asia — people who traditionally lived independent of government, economics, or surrounding cultures — the shock could well be devastating.

It seemed that the quilting operation added insult to injury. Here were talented needle artists who, along with all the other sacrifices, were expected to give up their native art for American quilting. Because I know what power quilting has over my fellow enthusiasts and myself — the joy and self-esteem it instills and the wonderful link to the past it provides — I realized that pa ndau had the same significance to my new friends. I promised that no matter what else might be lost to these gentle people, their native folk art would endure.

As a result, several new projects were created. The first was the production of pa ndau appliqué kits. We knew that American needle artists would want to sample this fascinating art form. And by providing them with folded and precut designs, we could make this craft easier for newcomers and benefit the Hmong at the same time. Best of all, it meant that the Hmong women could put down their quilting needles for a few hours a week so they could cut and baste pa ndau. How the room hums on the days we make kits! The women still need help in packaging kits and filling orders, but soon they will know enough English and fundamental business practices to supervise their own operations completely. They look forward to beginning a new, deluxe line of kits that will combine pa ndau and garment-making.

In the first year, the women have accomplished many exciting things. In addition to quilting techniques, they have learned the concepts of uniformity, quality control, and their responsibilities as a group. Many are now able to "talk shop" in English. The work force has diminished drastically as the women have moved in search of employment for their husbands. But as younger women join the group, they bring with them fluent English, skills in mathematics, and a hint of "business sense." Sickness and poverty continue to impede the women's efforts, but the Hmong are determined folk. Through the ups and downs, they have managed to sustain a cheerful attitude.

The newest project is funded by a grant designed to provide jobs for artists. Work is beginning now on a large wall hanging that will be offered for exhibition across the state of Iowa. Drawing on the talents of many needle artists, it will be a large rectangle with a starry sprinkling of pa ndau designs across panels of fabric representing the rainbow. It will focus attention on the story of the Hmong and embody the hope and quiet beauty these women know through their needlework.

It is said that hope for the Hmong lies in the new generation, that schooling and exposure to the American culture at an early age will speed assimilation into our society. With this assimilation, though, comes a loss of identity. And for the Hmong, this will be especially painful. But somehow the pain will be lessened if the tribal loyalty can remain and if the Hmong name can be recognized and respected. We hope that, by keeping pa ndau alive, we can preserve a link to the past and make the future shine brighter.

Pictured are the Cottage Quilters of Des Moines, Iowa. From left to right: May Yang, Sao Thao Lee, Chia Lor, Mao Thor Lee, and Carla Hassel. Not pictured: Chue Vang, Se Vang, and Mai Chao Vang.